Jeni Auchinleck
2 Castle Street
CRAIL.

Siamese Cats

SIAMESE CATS are the reigning
favourites of the cat world. Some
thousands of registrations are made
each year in Great Britain alone, while
in Australia, South Africa and the
U.S.A. their popularity increases yearly
in leaps and bounds.

For all Siamese lovers this is undoubtedly one of the most authoritative
and comprehensive books on SIAMESE
CATS ever written. The author,
an International show judge, and for
many years a successful breeder of
Siamese, with many Champions to
her name, has provided a first-class
introduction and guide for the pet
owner, as well as an invaluable
reference work for the serious breeder.

General Editor: CHRISTINA FOYLE

The cover illustration is of a litter bred
by Mrs. Mavis Dunn. *Left to right:* Wee-
One, Tarkas, Lady Fair, My Lovely,
Tobias and Blue Liz. Sire: Ch. Bluehayes
Foxy.

SIAMESE CATS

by

Kathleen R. Williams

Revised Edition

W. & G. FOYLE LIMITED

119-125 CHARING CROSS ROAD

LONDON, W.C.2

First published 1960

Reprinted 1970
Reprinted January 1971

© *W. & G. Foyle Limited, 1960*

Printed in Great Britain
by Rocastle, Leavesden, Watford, Herts.

Contents

List of Illustrations

FATE

*To 'Lob', the first Seal-Point
I ever owned.*

I fell in love with
    Your blue eyes;
That cold clear gaze
    Of ancient skies.
Your lovely grace,
    Your perfect poise;
Your devilish,
    Seagull-haunted noise.
I fell in love
    For the rest of my days
With Siamese cats
    And their heavenly ways.

E. VIVIEN EDMONDS

Introduction

HISTORY RECORDS the discovery of cats at about the same time as the horse, and most museums have drawings and records dating back to the past 2,000 years.

According to legend, cats were created in the Ark; one says that when Noah was asked, 'What security can there be for man or beast with the lion living amongst us?' Noah called upon the Most High, and upon the King of Beasts there descended a fever whereupon peace of mind was restored to the inhabitants of the Ark. However, Noah's attention was then drawn to the mouse who they said would eat their clothes and gnaw the wood. Once more Noah asked for guidance, and the lion sneezed and from his nostril ran a cat. Since then mice have been timid and hidden in holes. Another story tells how the pig spat forth a pair of rats, which were so prolific in their breeding that Noah was worried. He called for guidance whereupon the lion roared at the pig with such force that a cat came from his nostrils; the cat killed the rats and mice so that only a pair were left alive. Thus the cat became arrogant, and to discipline him Noah tied him to the bridge during a storm – hence his fear and dislike of water.

Cats have always played a part in the British way of life. As early as 948 we read that Howel the Good ordered that the price of a kitten, before it could see, was to be a penny; had it caught a mouse it was twopence, if more than one mouse the price rose to fourpence. He further ordered that any person who stole or killed a cat guarding his granaries must forfeit a milch ewe, its fleece and lamb – or as much wheat as, when poured on the cat held suspended by the tail with head touching the ground, would form a piled up heap to cover the top of the cat's tail.

The popularity of Siamese Cats knows no bounds and each year many new owners are captivated by their charms, not only in the British Isles but in many parts of the world. They give companionship and affection generously and expect affection and love in return. They are poems of movement and colour but remain a law unto themselves. They live happily domesticated, but their alertness and panther-like movement indicate their jungle background.

Once having *been owned* by a Siamese no other cat will suffice. Their origin is steeped in mystery, and it would provide an excellent brain exercise for lovers of Siamese Cats to delve into their history. It is generally accepted that they originated in Siam, but others opine that they are a mutation of the Indian cat, and yet others that they originated in Egypt. The Ancient Egyptians indicated their love for animals in their worship of animals of all kinds. The city of Babastes was set up and there the goddess Pashe was worshipped. In form she was depicted as a woman with the head of a cat.

Sir Compton Mackenzie says he cannot agree with the theory that there is a trace of the Egyptian Cat in the Siamese Cat. He is of the opinion that its only relative in Europe is the Manx Cat, whose ancestors may have been introduced by a homecoming sailor of long ago.

There must be many theories about their origin, but wherever they came from Siamese cat lovers are grateful for their wonderful fidelity and companionship.

CHAPTER ONE

History and Characteristics

THE SIAMESE CATS that live with us today are descendants of cats introduced into Great Britain about the year 1884. There are many theories, legends and stories about their origin but, as far as I am able to trace, there is no *written* record anywhere and their early history is still obscure.

I think the most likely theory is that the Royal Palace Cat of Siam was the product of a union between one of the domestic cats of Siam and the Egyptian Cat. What is known is that the Siamese as we know them today are descendants of cats brought to England from Siam in 1884. In *Mysteries of Religion and Magic*, M. Oldfield Howey says: 'For two hundred years Siamese Cats were only to be found in that portion of the Royal City of Bangkok where the monarch and his court resided, but though we can trace the variety for so long a period, its origin remains obscure. The Hon. Russell Gordon, who made a study of the subject, considers it is derived from a cross between the Sacred Cat of Burmah and the Annamite Cats that were introduced into the religiously sealed and guarded Burmese and Cambodian Empire of Khiner, when this succumbed to the attack of the Siamese and Annamites in the seventeenth century'.

Mr. Owen Gould, who was Consul General in Bangkok, Siam, brought the first Siamese Cat to England in the year 1884. Mrs. Veley, his sister, exhibited at the Crystal Palace Cat Show in 1895. This was the first Siamese Cat to be exhibited in England. About the year 1886, Mrs. Vyvyan succeeded in obtaining a pair of cats and two kittens from the palace in Bangkok and brought them to England.

Miss Forestier-Walker, daughter of General Walker, also brought one male and three females to England in the same year. The introduction of this new breed was an immediate success and in 1892 the first standard of points was published in *Our Cats*, under the heading of 'Points of Excellence for the Royal Cat of Siam', as given by Harrison Weir.

These cats imported between 1884 and 1887 formed the foundation stock from which most of the Siamese bred in England have been produced.

The Siamese Cat Club was formed in 1901 to improve the standard and protect the breed, and Siamese cat lovers today owe much to those pioneers who did so much in the early part of the century to improve the standard by intensive, selective breeding. The original standard of points was drawn up by the Siamese Cat Club in 1902 and compared with the new Standard of Points, issued by the Siamese Cat Club in 1958 (page 25) indicates the changes that have taken place over the years.

There are five different colours of Siamese Cats being bred in Britain today: Seal-pointed, Blue-pointed, Chocolate-pointed, Red-pointed and Lilac-pointed. I have no doubt that, in this age of experiment and change, further colours may be evolved.

The colours officially recognized are Seal-pointed, Blue-pointed and Chocolate-pointed.

The original Standard of Points for the Royal Siamese Cat, 1902, is as follows:

BODY COLOUR (20). As light and even as possible, cream being most desirable, but fawn also admissible, without streaks, bars, blotches, or any other body markings.

POINTS (15). i.e., mask, ears, legs, feet and tail, dark and clearly defined, of the shade known as 'seal' brown.

MASK (15). Complete, i.e. connected by tracings with the ears, neither separated by a pale ring (as in kittens), nor blurred and indistinct, the desideratum being to preserve the 'marten' face, an impression greatly aided by a good mark.

EYES (20). Bright and decided blue.

COAT (10). Glossy and close lying.

SHAPE (10). Body rather long, legs proportionately slight.

HEAD (10). Rather long and pointed.

> Any cat failing to obtain 75 of the above marks shall not be eligible for the Club challenge prize and medal.

GENERAL APPEARANCE. With points emphasized above, a somewhat curious and striking looking cat of medium size, if weighty, not showing bulk, as this would detract from the admired 'svelte' appearance. In type, in every particular the reverse of the ideal short-haired domestic cat, and with properly preserved contrasts in colour, a very handsome animal, often also distinguished by a kink in the tail.

REMARKS. While admitting that blue, blacks and whites and tabbies and other coloured cats may also be cats of Siam, these being common to all parts of the world, this Club recognizes only as Siamese cats, those cats the points of which conform to the above standard, and is, in fact, desirous of encouraging the breeding of those particular cats first made known to British fanciers as the 'royal' Siamese.

Many of the original Siamese Cats had kinks in their tails and a squint or cross eyes. These characteristics make the following legends interesting.

The kink in the tail came about because the Royal Princesses, when bathing, used their own cats' tails to hold their rings and the kinks developed to prevent the rings falling off.

Then there is the one about the squint. The Sacred Cats of the Temple were left by the priest to guard a valuable temple vase. This was guarded with such zeal that the steadfast staring at the vase caused the Cats' eyes to cross and their tails curled round the vase to become kinked. In *The Cat*, published in 1881, George Mivart says, 'The Royal Siamese Cat is one of uniform fawn colour, which may be of a very dark tinge. There is a tendency to a darker colour, about the muzzle, as in pug-dogs. It has also remarkable blue eyes and sometimes, at least, two bald spots on the forehead. It has a small head'.

During the past seventy-odd years, many changes have been brought about by selective breeding, and the following description of the present-day Siamese Cat embodied in the new Standard of Points issued by the Siamese Cat Club in 1958, indicates the changes that have taken place.

The Siamese Cat should be a beautifully balanced animal with head, ears and neck carried on a long svelte body, supported on fine legs and feet, with a tail in proportion. The head should be wedge shaped, neither round nor pointed, with straight profile; the mask complete connected by tracings with the ears (except in kittens),

*the eyes a deep blue (green tinge to be considered a fault). Expression
alert and intelligent.*

His type, shape, aloofness and panther-like movement reminds
one of the big wild jungle cats, but your Siamese has, for all his
aloofness, a devotion to his human family that few other animals
give. The Siamese is domesticated, a perfect companion in
sickness and health, for when you are ill he will understand well
and comfort one, not so much by a great deal of fuss and show of
affection, but by a quiet companionship that says: 'Cheer up,
all will be well'. Let me instance two Siamese who like to curl
around their owner's head when she rests – but should she have
a migraine headache, they lie at her side and are quite still,
giving a close feeling of companionship and sympathy that is
difficult to describe.

The conception that Siamese Cats are fierce is quite wrong.
There are such Siamese, of course. There are also bad-tempered
humans! In all breeds of animal, human or otherwise, one meets
bad temper. Siamese love children and get on with other animals.
Generally speaking they have gentle temperaments and are
friendly, if rather aloof, and very courageous. They have a
great sense of humour, as you will soon learn when you own one.

There is a story of a Siamese queen who taught herself a trick
with a rabbit paw – this trick she would perform for her own
amusement in her owner's presence. Often, when visitors were
sitting around the fire, she would bring in her rabbit paw. 'She
is going to do the trick of which I spoke', her owner would say –
but, after some show of being about to start, she would pick up
the rabbit paw and walk majestically out, with an expression
which said 'Had you that time'. It is this ability to speak with
look and movement that is one of their many charms.

Since 1945 the popularity of the Siamese Cat has increased
year by year and there are more people breeding today than ever
before.

What is their particular charm and why are so many people
attracted to Siamese Cats? I think perhaps the first thing that
holds one's attention is the complete contrast between Siamese
and other Short-Hair Breeds. The colouring is so different – the
pale body, dark mask, dark points on the legs and tail; then the
long, svelte body, beautiful slim legs and long whip tail – and, of

course, the amazing shape and colour of the eyes. The eyes are oriental in shape and a wonderful brilliant deep blue in colour. The balanced appearance given by this combination is so marked that it creates a lasting impression. When one has acquired a Siamese cat or kitten, it is their character, conversational chatter, remarkable intelligence and almost human affection which exercises a permanent fascination over their owner.

CHAPTER TWO

The Five Points

SEAL-POINTED SIAMESE

THE GENERAL APPEARANCE of the Seal-Pointed we know today is one of svelte polished sleekness, with well balanced body of good proportion, fine slim legs and small oval feet, the hind legs being slightly higher than the front. The head should have good width between the eyes (not too broad for the length), narrowing in a straight line to the muzzle; often this is described as a wedge head. There are different types of wedge. Drawings which follow will indicate my meaning.

THREE TYPES OF HEADS

Head A shows a rather long, well-balanced muzzle; B is slightly shorter but still well-balanced; Head C needs more length.

These sketches are to guide and explain type, as regards head shape.

The ears should be on the large side, wide at the base.

Tail long and tapering (whip like).

The eyes should be a very definite blue, shining clear and oriental in shape.

Although oriental in shape, the eyes are not so much slit in appearance as originally seen. Possibly the more open eye has developed because the sunlight is not so intense in this country, as in the tropics. The placement must still be oriental, not round.

Points, that is, colour on legs, paws, tail and ears should be a good seal brown which, lying flat and close, has the appearance of black. The body colour to be cream, shading to fawn, the texture fine, short and lying close, which gives that perfect glossy finished appearance.

BLUE-POINTED SIAMESE

In type and shape Blue-Pointed Siamese Cats are the same as the Seal-Pointed; they differ only in colour (the points) that is mask, legs, ears and tail, being blue. The body colour glacial white, shading gradually into blue on the back, the same cold tone as points, but of lighter blue. The eyes clear, bright, vivid blue. According to the records, the first Blue-Pointed Siamese was exhibited in 1890, but the judge refused to recognize it at the time as a Siamese.

There was a suggestion that, as Blue-Pointed males were inclined to be heavy, an allowance should be made for this when judging, but the standard is quite clear on this, as you will see on page 26. As a judge and breeder, I think much confusion would be caused by any variation of standard for one colour.

Was the Blue Point the result of pure breeding, appearing as a 'sport' or was it the offspring of a mating with another breed? There seems to be no record. It has been suggested that the Blue Point was the result of mating a Siamese with a Korat cat, which is short-haired and lavender.

Mrs. G. Hindley, Major and Mrs. J. C. Rendall, and the late Mrs. Grace Cox-Ife did much to improve the breed in the early days of their introduction.

Much could be written about the breeding of Blue Point to Blue Point, but in this book it is proposed to give you the bare facts. Blue Points bred to Blue Points tend, at the moment, to produce rather heavier types. There are exceptions, and Blue Points are definitely today nearer Seal Point type than ever before.

A Seal-Pointed male and female both having Blue Point ancestry can produce Blue Points. A Blue-Pointed Stud mated to a Seal-Pointed Queen, and vice versa, can produce Blue-Pointed and Seal-Pointed kittens in the same litter, provided both adults carry the Blue Point factor. Difficulty is being experienced in obtaining the glacial white coat. But I have no doubt breeders will overcome this, given time.

CHOCOLATE-POINTED SIAMESE

The standard for type and shape is the same for all Siamese Cats; the difference is in the colour. The points being the colour of milk chocolate, the body colouring ivory all over, shading to the colour of the points. Eyes – clear, bright, vivid blue.

Although the Chocolate-Pointed Siamese was known as far back as 1900, the Chocolate-Pointed Cat was not officially recognized until many years later. In the early days some cross-breeding was attempted; this caused the Siamese Cat Club Committee to issue the letter printed below:

> The committee of the Siamese Cat Club wish to draw attention to the unfortunate diversity of opinion concerning Siamese Cats expressed in articles which appear from time to time in some of the papers which devote a portion of their issue to cat news. One great object of the Siamese Club is to encourage the distinct breeding of the royal cat of Siam and also the chocolate cat of Siam – both beautiful in their own way, but recognized as distinct breeds. The Siamese Club is young, and not infallible, but containing as it does most of the principal breeders and exhibitors, its committee would like to record their opinions on some few points which have appeared in the Press, in order to avoid a silence which might be construed as consent with

regard to colour. They cannot agree that a royal can be too light in body colour, nor can they endorse 'we like a nice cream body, chocolate saddle and the points glossy black, shading away to chocolate'. Another paper advises the mating of royal Siamese with the chocolate variety. It is true that the young kittens are very pretty, but after six months old, quickly become dark and blurred. The great beauty of royal Siamese is the contrast between the sharply defined, deepest brown markings and a body of as light a cream as possible.

A third paper gives the information that an exhibitor, known to it, has bred prize winning Siamese from a cross between a white cat with blue eyes and a Siamese queen. It also mentions another case where such crossing has produced good Siamese kittens, and thinks 'that many other people have with more or less success followed the same tactics'. The above experiment has often been tried, purposely and accidentally, but no case is known to the writer where the result has been anything like Siamese, the kittens always favouring the English parent. All Siamese are born white, and therefore if the children of one white parent died quite young, such a mistake might be natural. It certainly would be very unfair to sell such kittens, as their progeny would inherit, and might pass on, an English parentage not even necessarily white. A white is, or may be, merely an albino variety.

Signed: *A. Forestier-Walker, Jean A. Spencer, May Robinson, L. Parker-Brough, S. F. Beckhouse, Constance Carew Cox.*

Amongst the early Chocolate Points enthusiasts, the late Miss F. Wentworth Fitzwilliam and Mrs. L. French, both well-known fanciers in their day, did much to promote the breed in the early 'thirties and it is from this stock that the present-day Chocolate Point is descended.

Miss Val Prentis also did much to encourage the breeding of Chocolate Points in the late 'thirties. Her female 'Georgina' was well known; it was through her that I became interested in Chocolate-Pointed Siamese. In post-war years I was fortunate enough to breed the first *all*-Chocolate Point litter.

In recent years more Chocolate Points have been **bred but** there is still plenty of room for improvement. Type has improved and colour, but not together; often the good-type kitten has too pale points. However, breeders of Chocolate Points are not deterred, they believe they will eventually achieve both type and colour in the same animal.

LILAC-POINTED SIAMESE

(Mrs. A. Hargreaves, F.R.Z., who bred the first Lilac-Pointed Siamese in England, has very kindly contributed this article on the breed.)

There are four natural colours in the Siamese cat – seal, chocolate, blue and lilac. Lilac-Pointed Siamese have been established in the United States for some years, but the first in Britain were born in 1955 in my cattery. They were among a litter of Blue Points and both parents were Blue Points. They came as a surprise to me because I had no idea any of my Siamese cats carried the necessary hereditary factors. It is, of course, possible that Lilac Points have been born in England before, remaining unrecognized, possibly thought to be very pale Blue Points. Also, unlike mine which are pure bred, they can be produced by out-crossing Siamese to other cats which possess the required colour combination.

Genetically the lilac colour is produced by a double dose of blue and chocolate, that is each parent must hand on to the kittens both blue and chocolate. No one can expect a complete litter of Lilac Points unless both parents are Lilac Points. If the parents happen to be Blue or Chocolate Points carrying the alternative colour there is a chance of about half the litter being Lilac Points, but with combinations of blue, chocolate and seal, the proportion will be much smaller.

These cats have delicate lilac-grey points, pink pads to their feet, faded rose nose leather, and their usually vivid blue eyes contrast well with their almost white body colouring. In fact they are the antithesis of the Seal Point, resembling the pastel tints of spring, while the latter are of the richer autumn shades. People who like their pets in pairs should have one of each, and will find the contrast delightful.

Lilac mated to lilac is, strangely, the only Siamese which can be relied upon to breed one hundred per cent true to colour.

All the other varieties *might* have inherited ancestral factors which are not visible and have not yet appeared in their kittens, and never will unless the appropriate mating takes place. However, a large number will undoubtedly always breed true.

So far there have been very few female Lilac Points born but Mrs. K. R. Williams is lucky in owning one which she has mated to a well-known Lilac Point Stud. Consequently she is the first breeder in England to possess an entire litter of Lilac-Pointed Siamese.

RED-POINTED SIAMESE

(Dr. Nora Archer, who has kindly contributed this section, pioneered Red Points in this country some years ago.)

It is interesting to reflect that nearly twenty years has passed by since Mrs. Rolling, of New York, first bred a recognized Red-Pointed Siamese Cat. Since then, we know of two other strains that have arisen from chance matings between red or cream males and Seal-Pointed Siamese queens; while several interested breeders both in U.S.A., Britain and South Africa have each developed their own carefully planned strain of this delightful new breed.

In appearance the Red-Pointed Siamese is a most distinctive study in gold, white and blue: the points colour is deep guinea gold, the body colour is very white, and the eye colour is sapphire blue. Like all other cats which demonstrate their possession of the Siamese factor, Red Points are born pure white and subsequently develop point colour in kittenhood. The Red Point, being pure both for red coloration and the Siamese colour restriction factors, is a true breeding variety: when Red Point is mated with Red Point, only Red-Pointed kittens result.

The new breed has come about by the combination in one animal, in the first instance by chance, and subsequently by design, of the red colour as seen in the red tabby, or red self, or the tortoise-shell, with the restriction of colour to the points as seen in the Siamese. This is an entirely new departure in Siamese cats, and something of an achievement, since the other accepted points colours alternative to seal, namely, blue and chocolate, are merely modifications of seal (that is, black), whereas red is a colour in its own right, genetically quite distinct from black.

Both the red colour and the Siamese distribution of colour are passed on from parent cats to their kittens as separate and independent characters according to a regular and clearly understood pattern. When a red male cat mates a black female, the female kittens possess the colour of both parents and will be tortoise-shell, while the male kittens inherit colour only from their mother and will be black. If the black female cat in question also happens to be pure for the Siamese factor, or as we should more commonly call her, is a Seal-Pointed queen, this has no obvious effect on the colour of the kittens: but in actual fact every one of them carries a Siamese factor, and when suitably mated, can itself produce Siamese offspring. If one of these tortoise-shell kittens is mated, when mature, to a Seal-Pointed Siamese male, she can produce from this mating six different varieties of kitten, among which is the Red-Pointed male. A red female cat can only result from a mating when red is present in both parents. This is equally true, or one might say doubly true, of the Red-Pointed female cat. Only when both parents show red and both at least carry Siamese factors, can a Red Point female kitten appear in a litter.

It will be seen from this brief summary of the technique of red-point breeding that at least four generations of carefully planned mating are required before a breeder can hope to obtain both female and male red-points. As has already been said, a number of interested breeders are at work. Although the breed has not yet received the official recognition of a breed number, the co-operation of these breeders is able to produce in the near future an established breed of high quality.

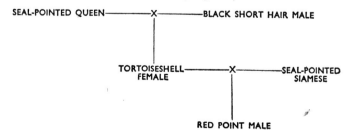

SEAL-POINTED QUEEN————————X————————BLACK SHORT HAIR MALE

TORTOISESHELL————————X————————SEAL-POINTED
FEMALE   SIAMESE

RED POINT MALE

CHAPTER THREE

The Siamese Cat Club and Standard of Points

THE SIAMESE CAT CLUB was founded in 1901 to promote the pure breeding of Siamese Cats, to draw up a Standard of Points for Siamese Cats, to select specialist judges of Siamese Cats and to organize and support Shows for the exhibition of Siamese Cats and Kittens. Sir Compton Mackenzie, the Club's President, has done much to encourage interest in the breed. He has been owned by Siamese Cats for many years! Since its inception, the Standard of Points has been revised from time to time, to cope with the continuing improvement in the breed. The present Standard of Points was revised in 1958.

For many years this was the only Club representing the Breed – however the past fifteen years has seen many changes, general interest in the Breed has increased, there are many more breeders and with this expansion, new clubs have come into being.

At the present time, there are six Clubs or Societies representing Siamese Cats; basically the objects of all the Clubs are the same, to improve the standard and to guarantee classes for members at the various shows.

*VALUE AND STANDARD OF POINTS
FOR THE SIAMESE CAT, 1958*

Seal-Pointed:
Value of Points:

(TYPE AND SHAPE, 50)
(Head, 15)
(Ears, 5)
(Eyes, 5)
(Body, 15)
(Legs and Paws, 5)
(Tail, 5)

Medium in size, body long and svelte, legs proportionately slim, hind legs slightly higher than front ones, feet small and oval, tail long and tapering (straight or slightly kinked at the extremity). Head long and well proportioned with width between the eyes, narrowing in perfectly straight lines to a fine muzzle. Ears rather large and pricked, wide at the base.

25

(COLOUR, 50)	Brilliant deep blue, shape oriental and slanting towards the nose. No squint.
(Eyes, 15)	
(Body Colour, 10)	Cream, shading gradually into pale warm fawn on the back.
(Points, 10)	
(Texture of Coat, 10)	Kittens paler in colour.
(Condition, 5)	Mask, ears, legs, feet and tail dense and clearly defined seal brown. Mask complete and (except in kittens) connected by tracings with the ears.
(TOTAL: 100)	Very short and fine in texture, glossy and close lying.

Blue-Pointed

The Standard is the same as for Seal-Pointed with the following exceptions:
Colour. Points: Blue, the ears, mask, legs, paws and tail to be the same colour. The ears should not be darker than the other points.
Eyes. Clear: Bright vivid blue.
Body. Body Colour: Glacial white, shading gradually into blue on back, the same cold tone as the points but of a lighter shade.
Texture of Coat. The same as for Seal-Pointed.

Chocolate-Pointed

The Standard is the same as for Seal-Pointed with the following exceptions:
Colour. Points: Milk chocolate, the ears, mask, legs, paws and tail to be the same colour. The ears should not be darker than the other points.
Eyes. Clear: Bright vivid blue.
Body. Ivory colour all over. Shading, if at all, to be to colour of points.
Texture of Coat. The same as for Seal-Pointed.

Lilac-Pointed

The Standard is the same as for Seal-Pointed with the following exceptions:
Eyes. Clear bright vivid blue.

Points. Frosty grey of pinkest tone.
Nose Leather and Pads. Faded lilac.
Body colour. Frosty white shading, if any, to tone with points.
Texture. As for all Siamese.

NOTES AND DEFINITIONS:

Definition of Squint: When the eyes are so placed that they appear to look permanently at the nose.

Notes: The Siamese Cat should be a beautifully balanced animal with head, ears and neck carried on a long svelte body, supported on fine legs and feet, with a tail in proportion. The head should be wedge shaped, neither round nor pointed, with straight profile; the mask complete connected by tracings with the ears (except in kittens), the eyes a deep blue (green tinge to be considered a fault). Expression alert and intelligent. White toes or toe to automatically disqualify an exhibit.

It is important to note that the Standard with regard to Type and Shape is the same for all Siamese Cats.

CHAPTER FOUR

General Management

I THINK PERHAPS the word 'management' is a misnomer! One does not own or manage a Siamese cat in the sense that he can be trained or dominated in any way. A dog can be trained and will obey the command of his owner – not so the Siamese cat. So – if you contemplate purchasing a Siamese cat, it is just as well to start off on the right foot so to speak, and fully appreciate that in due time your Siamese will own you!

When Siamese cats were first brought into this country, they were often kept in semi-tropical conditions. This, and the variations in the British climate, caused many deaths; the mortality rate became high and the belief that Siamese were delicate caused a sharp decline in their popularity.

Thanks to the knowledge and experience passed on by breeders over the past sixty years, the Siamese cats bred today are not in the least delicate and they are well able to withstand the British climate; in fact British-bred Siamese are in great demand overseas and are exported to most countries. Nobody who has lived with a Siamese cat and experienced their fidelity, humour and affection can have the same regard for any other animal. Remember, your Siamese is an individualist; each one is different. They have individual likes and dislikes. They are self-reliant, but they need human love and companionship. They are greedy and will steal food from under your very nose. They are sometimes inclined to be destructive but when their virtues are set against their faults, they far outweigh them.

Siamese cats are carnivorous animals and flesh in some form or another should be used in the bulk of their meals. Small bones can cause much trouble and should always be removed from the rabbit, meat or poultry before it is fed. They like a varied diet and look for their meals at regular intervals. Unfinished meals should not be left lying about; they can be contaminated by flies and cause disease. If your kitten likes milk, give him milk. As a general rule Siamese prefer water;

milk is inclined to make their motions loose – you must be the judge of whether it is good for him or not.

A bowl of fresh water should always be available. This should be changed daily. It is also important that the water bowl should always be in the same place. Most animals like grass; in many cases it is an essential part of their diet, but cats seem to use it as a remedy for their digestive troubles; the particular type of grass they require is selected by instinct. Shortly after eating grass they often vomit it; this seems to act like magic. After they have eaten grass, cats that seemed off colour will appear full of beans. If you live in a flat or do not possess a garden, grass can be grown in pots or bowls. The particular type of couch grass essential to cats can be obtained from the Cats' Protection League, 29 Church Street, Slough. Full particulars regarding cultivation are printed on the packet.

Cats are naturally clean; when quite young they are taught by their mother to use the sanitary tray provided for her use. As they grow the kittens look for a tray, and if you have not provided one do not blame the kittens for their accidents. Although they clean themselves daily, Siamese love to be groomed; regular brushing and grooming will keep both the cat and the coat in good condition. Warning! Do not brush too hard and take all the undercoat out. Cats also like the feel of a comb. When taking the comb from head to tail you will often find a ripple of skin as the comb approaches the tail – to remedy this take the loose skin at the neck and hold forward; the comb will then make a clear run from neck to tail. A rubber brush will quickly collect loose hairs, but be careful you are not too strenuous with brushes of any kind. If you use any kind of bristle brush, see that the bristles are short and not too hard. The best way to groom is with the hand. Curve the hand and draw quickly and firmly from head to tail. As the hand leaves the tail, loose hairs will fall to the ground.

Cats keep their claws in condition by scratching. In their wild state, I expect, they made regular use of trees. Now that they are domesticated, Siamese use furniture, but they generally settle for one chair. To preserve one's furniture, and because I believe they prefer them, it is well to provide clawing blocks or boards. A clawing block is a piece of soft wood 4 in. by 4 in. which should be the length of an adult cat's body, so that both front and back legs can be on the wood. The upright scratching block is made on the same principal, but must be firmly wedged, or set in a solid base. A piece of carpet tied round the leg of a kitchen table, or an old ironing board on end against the wall, will also serve the same purpose.

Some cats' claws grow quicker than others and if you do not want to file or cut them yourself, make regular visits to your vet. If you use a file, it must be of the heavy type used in carpentry, *not* a nail file. In some countries, de-clawing cats has been suggested, even done. In great Britain it is not favoured and much discussion has taken place 'for' and 'against' this practice. My personal feeling would be that it should NOT be done. A cat's claws are both useful for climbing, holding food and, if need be, in defence. The claws which are provided by nature should *not* be removed.

Siamese like travelling about with their owners. They travel quite well in motor cars and can quickly be trained to a lead. If you take a cat on a journey, it is essential to have a cat basket or, better still, a box. Although a cat may be well used to its owner, sudden fright could cause it to dash away. In any case it is much more comfortable for a cat to be settled in a basket or box. If baskets are used in the winter, they should be covered on the outside with thick paper to protect the cat from draughts. So, on the whole, perhaps the best kind of container would be a cat box made of plywood or similar material.

Travelling by car, a collar, harness and lead is advisable. Your cat is then always ready to leave the car with you under control. By the way see that you have a sanitary tray in the car and don't feed just before taking your cat on a journey.

If you have to send your cat unaccompanied by rail, see that she is comfortably settled in a box or basket free from draught. Label clearly; see that the consigner's name and telephone number are both clearly stated, as well as the station of destination. The box or basket should be large enough for the cat's comfort and no more. If the container is too large it can be just as uncomfortable as if it were too small. There should be height enough for the cat to stand upright and turn round. Make sure it is properly secured and have a Livestock Label affixed and if possible hand it to the guard of the train yourself.

It is advisable, wherever possible, to send by through train –

where a change has to be made notify the Station Master at the station where the change is to be made, at least two days beforehand. He will then see that your cat is not delayed.

It would, I think, be true to say that there are hundreds, perhaps thousands, of Siamese cats living in flats both in London and the provinces. In London it is quite usual to see Siamese cats being exercised on leads in London parks and open spaces. If a kitten between say three and four months is fitted with a harness and lead and exercised daily, he soon becomes accustomed to it. The most suitable collar to start is an elastic one which allows freedom without strain. Having fitted the kitten with the harness, do not attempt to direct his movement. You let him become used to the new experience, and be prepared to devote a little time and perhaps much patience to the job. The kitten will soon respond and you will be well-rewarded for your trouble. Some kittens take to the lead at once; others sit down like a puppy, but soon learn. Adults should have a soft leather collar with an elastic inset.

Siamese can live anywhere with owners to whom they are devoted. Friends of mine live on a Thames sailing barge. One of their kittens appeared in 'Raising a Riot', which was filmed near their mooring. All the cats were interested in the water and all that went on in the creek. They were fascinated by passing waves. One of their kittens, who was sold to a vicarage with a large garden, disliked it so much he had to come back; he obviously preferred life afloat!!

Ornamental Ponds and your Pet

Friends of mine lost a very dear Siamese named Artie. Artie progressed well as a kitten, but as he grew older was always having sore throats, ulcerated tongue, swollen glands, liver disorders – and finally died. The post-mortem showed that the liver was a complete solid mass of fibrous tissue, probably caused by a chemical. It was found that copper sulphate, used to keep ornamental ponds clear, was the likely cause and it explained the long, intermittent illnesses. There is no need to use any dangerous chemical to clear garden ponds. Permanganate of potash will do the trick, or, if you want something ready prepared you can use Clarox; the makers assure me that it is harmless to animals who drink the water.

Wool Eaters

Fortunately kittens that develop this habit are few and far between. The only cure to my knowledge is to keep wool out of your pet's way; this may cure his desire of it. Various reasons have been put forward from time to time. Lack of mineral salts! Lack of calcium! Lack of something unspecified! I do remember one lady writing to me saying she had cured her kitten with definite concentrated doses of calcium. Alas, this was not a cure – the improvement was short lived. There is no answer! Is it possibly boredom? What about a bad habit like a child biting his nails? Certainly try giving extra vitamins and calcium tablets, but do, at the same time, remove all temptation. Use cotton blankets for his bed; although these are 'woolly-ish', they do not seem to have the same appeal. If your pet even starts to lick these, take the blanket away and give him newspaper. I have known this to effect a cure, the patience of the owner and the intelligence of her pet together obtaining the desired result.

Pedigrees

Many people think, because an animal has a pedigree, it is the best of its kind. This is of course quite wrong. A pedigree is a chart of ancestry or family tree. It certainly means that the animal is pure bred, but in Siamese cats whether it is one of the best of its kind would depend on its points, type and shape, etc. It is always wise to have a pedigree with your kitten. Then you know it is pure bred, and, whatever its type, a Siamese is always a wonderful pet and companion.

Boarding

The companionship of humans is essential to the happiness and welfare of Siamese Cats, so if you have to find a home for your cat while on holidays, make sure the owner understands Siamese Cats and can give them the attention they require. There are many boarding establishments these days, some of them have been built specially for housing cats, giving space, light, air, and with wired runs from the living quarters, so that your pet has plenty of fresh air and controlled freedom. Some of these cater for Siamese Cats only. If you are able to do so, it is as well to pay the one you select, a visit, to satisfy yourself that your cat will have every comfort during your absence.

'Dare I?' A Study of Brackledown Blue Sky; sire Ch. Bluehayes Foxy, dam Brackledown Beauty. Owned by Mrs. Tilt and bred by Mrs. E. Morrison.

Pr. Johnny Gurkha and Caliban, bred by Mrs. M. Horwood. Their sire is Ch. Sabukia Sir Galahad.

Are stud cats gentle? Mrs. Elizabet Eytzinger's stud International Ch. Doneraile Leo is pictured with some of his offspring, and (below) a portrait of Leo's magnificent head.

Marriage Lines

A clergyman purchased a kitten sired by one of my studs, and in due course brought her to be mated. He and his family were great cat lovers, hence we talked rather long when they came to collect the queen. They went off (with, of course, the pedigree of the stud which is given when a queen is mated). In a short while he was back and the following conversation took place:

'I'm so sorry to trouble you, but I don't think this form is complete.'

I looked at it. 'Perfectly alright', said I.

'But it only has the mate's name on it. My queen is not mentioned.'

I explained that he already had the pedigree of the queen and when the kittens arrived, these two pedigrees formed the kittens' pedigree.

'Ah!', said he, 'how foolish of me! I am so used to issuing Marriage Certificates that it seemed natural to look for the male and female on the form!'

How delightful these incidents are and how very many of them make new and lasting friends – all through Siamese cats.

A prefix is a cattery name or distinguishing mark. For instance my prefix is 'Doneraile' and cats bearing that prefix are guaranteed pure-bred and are from my cattery.

During my life, I have found the most interesting and exciting things happen at the oddest moments. Owing to a show date having to be changed at short notice, I found I had two judging engagements in one week. Returning from Dublin by air, I had just a day at home before entraining for the North. Taking a taxi at Victoria Station, I must have sighed rather wearily as I heaved myself into the taxi. 'You sound weary', said the taxi driver. 'I am', said I, 'all because I love cats.' 'Cats', he said, '*I* love cats. A cat was the cause of my playing the piano.' 'Sounds interesting' said I, 'How so?' 'Well', he replied, 'it started when I was a kid. My father got very fed up with me sitting nursing our old black cat in the evenings, and decided, if I wanted to sit, I should do so to some advantage. He bought a piano, at which I'm now no mean player, but I still nursed our old cat. Now I'm married the wife doesn't care for cats, so we've settled for a goldfish!'

CHAPTER FIVE

Buying a Kitten

WHEN YOU DECIDE you would like a Siamese kitten, don't rush to the nearest pet shop simply because, like many other folk, you cannot wait, and so buy the first kitten you see. Be patient, don't rush, find out something about the breed and contact a reliable breeder. There are many of them and they are always willing to help you.

Well, here we are, and there are the kittens! After their first surprise at seeing somebody new to them, most healthy kittens will start to play again, without any sign of nervousness. Apart from its points, when buying a kitten it is well to know what to look for. The nose should be moist, the ears clean, eyes bright and alert, the mouth a healthy pink and the kitten should have the general appearance of lively health. You must accept advice from the breeder unless you have some knowledge of Siamese. If you think the advice foolish, never mind, follow it, at least until you have gained some knowledge of your own kitten.

From nine to ten weeks old is a good age to purchase a kitten. No definite age can be laid down as kittens vary, some are very forward at seven to eight weeks, even earlier.

Kittens do not always fulfil their promise and an outstanding kitten can be a disappointment as an adult. If you decide beforehand whether you intend to breed or have the kitten neutered, the breeder can help you in your choice. Kittens need and enjoy affection and companionship; do not buy a kitten unless you intend to fulfil these needs.

When you go to see a litter of kittens, it sometimes happens that one particular kitten will attach itself to you, in which case that is your kitten; no other will be quite the same to you.

If you are wanting a pet, do not be too influenced by a wonderful pedigree. Indeed, when purchasing a kitten for showing, both the kitten's, dam's and sire's pedigrees should be taken into consideration. It is always best to be advised by a breeder of repute.

When you take your new kitten home, remember that different voices and new surrounding are strange to him. It is most important to follow the diet given by the breeder. DO NOT OVERFEED. Decide where you are going to put the toilet tray, where he is going to be fed and the place for his water bowl – and stick to these. Do not over-fuss him. Let him find his way about and inquire into all corners, pieces of furniture, etc. When he is tired he will come to you to settle down.

Generally speaking let the kitten have a free run, but don't encourage him when he tries to run up your back and sit on your neck. It is amusing and adorable in kittens, but when 6 lb. of cat climbs up it is not so amusing, and if you allow your kitten to do this it is unfair to expect him not to do so when he grows up.

Start off with the toilet tray in the place you mean to keep it. If you move it around, you cannot blame your kitten if he uses the different places. He merely thinks you have forgotten to put the pan there.

I once sent a kitten of $3\frac{1}{2}$ months to a new home some distance away. I had a telephone call to say that, just after arrival, the kitten had rushed quite madly up the curtains and was sitting on the pelmet, spitting. What could they do? Having calmed my caller down a little, I asked exactly what had happened – on arrival the kitten had jumped out of the basket and found the toilet tray. He would not eat, but the new owner had cuddled him; however he seemed to want to get down. Finally he struggled free, rushed to the curtain to escape. Yes, escape, for the new owner had not taken into consideration that, to the kitten, everything was strange. He just wanted to look round the new home and her enforced embrace infuriated him.

My advice was to behave normally, ignore the kit, but, without looking at him, keep up a running conversation with him, on no account to approach him, but to sit, when he descended, until he came to her. Later the husband telephoned to say the kitten was asleep in his wife's lap. When dealing with cats or kittens, do try to put yourself in their place and use your common sense.

Kittens, and cats for that matter, like to have a good look round, and sniff at all the furniture; once that is done they feel they know where everything is and can run to hide if they need to do so. Kittens or cats when going to a new home, having looked round and smelt everything, decide on a base. From this they set forth on their voyages of discovery and run back with great speed whenever in doubt or apprehensive. So, when introducing a kitten, let her have the run of at least the rooms in which she is going to live at first, particularly the living rooms where she will spend most of her time. The newcomer is then not at the disadvantage of not knowing where the furniture is placed.

If you are introducing a kitten to an adult, it may take to the kitten at once, or it may not. In any case I would suggest they are left alone; they will soon get used to one another. DO NOT hold each cat and let them sniff at one another; that each is restrained will set them in doubt of one another. Undoubtedly there may be spittings but usually newcomers are accepted in a few days.

SIAMESE NAMES FOR SIAMESE CATS

AAPORN – ornament.
AAREE – generosity
AAWUT – weapon.
CHAISAI – innocent.
CHAISEE – victory.
CHAWALIT –
CHITR – mind.
CHONGRAK – faithful.
CHUI CHAI – gait, a Siamese dance.
DOK BAN YEN – petunia-like flower.
DOK MAI – flower of a plant.
DOK PHI SUA – carnation.
KRAISEE – lion.
KRIANG SAK – full of power.
KOHSOOM – lotus.
MONGKOL –
MONGKUT – crown.
NILLA – jet (black).
OHPAS – sunlight.
OODOM – plenteous.

OOT'AI –
PAKDEE – faithful.
PRANEE – kindness.
RATSMEE – glory.
RITTEE – power.
SAHKON – universe.
SAMPAN – to bind.
SAMUTRA – ocean.
SAWAT – fortune.
SOHPAR – handsome.
SOOPARP – polite.
TANORM – with care.
TAWEE –
TITAYA – sun.
VAREE – river.
WARAH – cat.
WILA – feline.
WINAI – discipline.
YI KHENG – crepe myrtle.
YINDEE – pleasure.
YOD RAK – beloved.

CHAPTER SIX

The Brood Queen

IF YOU ARE THINKING of breeding Siamese Cats to make money, I would advise you to reconsider, because breeding pedigree cats is not the same as breeding pedigree dogs. Breeding Siamese is just a fascinating hobby, whereas the breeding of pedigree dogs can be a commercial proposition. You cannot give your cats the food, time, energy and attention that is necessary if you have to count the cost. However, if you are fond of animals, and cats in particular, there is no more rewarding hobby than breeding Siamese Cats. They love human companionship; each one is an individualist. They all believe in free speech, and, when they want to talk, express themselves freely; they are completely self-reliant and independent, and finally a 'calling' queen has to be heard to be believed; the nearest equivalent is the constant crying of a young baby. A queen can call for the first time as early as four months or, as from my experience, as late as 18 months. Nobody – I repeat 'nobody', can tell how long this period of calling will last; it varies. It may only last for five days or it may go on for weeks on end, but I am thankful to say that this is very rare.

Remember if you want to breed good stock, you must obtain a well-bred female kitten. Do not buy a kitten because it is less expensive than a better one, thinking that you can mate it to a good stud, and thus produce a super kitten. A good stud cannot rectify all the faults of your queen.

The object of all breeders should be the breeding of stock to the Standard of Points laid down by the Siamese Cat Club. Don't be unduly influenced by Show Awards; remember the best cats do not all get into the Show pens, and Show Awards can be misleading to the novice who may not understand the difference between 'OPEN' and 'SIDE' classes.

Study the Standard of Points; get to know them off by heart; try and breed to them; then, when you are looking at Siamese, whether at Shows, at a friend's or your own kittens, you will always have perfection in mind, and so make a valuable contribution to the breeding of the perfect Siamese Cat, for which we all strive.

A good brood queen is far more important than a winning queen; it is not always your winner on the Show bench that produces winning stock, and blood lines should be carefully considered before you mate your queen. Study the pedigrees and make sure both cats do not carry the same faults.

In due course she calls, let us say at six months; do not mate her then. If possible wait until she is nine, ten or twelve months old, but, should she call very frequently after her first, early call, it is better to mate her, provided she is in good health and a reasonable size, otherwise the constant calling may retard her development. In some cases cysts on the ovaries develop in later life – it is quite possible that these are caused through early frustration.

Normally there will be no doubt in your mind when your queen calls. Some are more vocal than others. At the start she will become more affectionate. Many people are at first puzzled by this display of affection and the antics of rolling and pushing along the ground – all this is part of the natural sequence of being 'in season'.

At any of these signs keep her indoors and under observation, for they are quick to find any small window or door left open for a second. Any moment she may start the Siamese love song, which varies from a persistent cry in all keys to a loud angry bark.

Kittens become adults at nine months. If your queen has been mated before she reaches adult age she should not be allowed to rear a large litter, otherwise the strain on her system may have a detrimental effect on her in later life. Four is a reasonable litter. A foster-mother can often be found to take the remainder of the litter. Whatever the size of the litter, you should relieve the strain on your queen by feeding the kittens a little at three weeks.

'Calling' may not cease immediately after she has been mated, she must be kept indoors until it has ceased. After mating, it is most important that the queen should be quiet a few days.

Nothing has been found that will definitely keep off prowling tom cats, who seem to sense any 'calling' queen within a mile. However, Eucalyptus Oil, rubbed on rump, legs and shoulders, is a deterrent to the local prowling tom. If you are sending to stud and have used this, you would, of course, well wash off before despatching her. The idea is really only for those of you who live in areas where un-neutered males abound.

The period of gestation is sixty-three to sixty-five days (nine weeks). Few Siamese have their litters on time; they are usually a few days overdue. I have known many cases where litters have not been born until seven, eight, even ten days after the due date. The queen and her family will be much more comfortable in a properly prepared maternity box. Having had several sizes and designs, I find one 14½ in. high, with flap which lifts, in order to help the queen if need be, and curtain in front, is very convenient. Made of hardboard and painted in enamel, it is easily thoroughly disinfected.

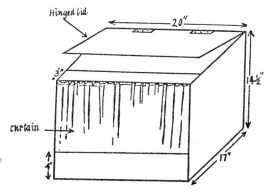

A suggested design for a maternity box.

Do not feed your queen extra food at once. In fact it is a big mistake to overfeed her during pregnancy. You do not want huge kittens or to upset the young mother's digestion. Her organs are not designed to digest more food than is needed. Of course, as the kittens develop, say at four weeks, food can be increased. Again, in the last week, do not overfeed and remember to give medicated paraffin or olive oil each day.

Calcium and Vitamin D are most important. Calcium needs Vitamin D to help its absorption into the blood stream and can

GESTATION CHART

Served January	Due March	Served February	Due April	Served March	Due May	Served April	Due June	Served May	Due July	Served June	Due August	Served July	Due September	Served August	Due October	Served September	Due November	Served October	Due December	Served November	Due January	Served December	Due February
1	5	1	5	1	3	1	3	1	3	1	3	1	2	1	3	1	3	1	3	1	3	1	2
2	6	2	6	2	4	2	4	2	4	2	4	2	3	2	4	2	4	2	4	2	4	2	3
3	7	3	7	3	5	3	5	3	5	3	5	3	4	3	5	3	5	3	5	3	5	3	4
4	8	4	8	4	6	4	6	4	6	4	6	4	5	4	6	4	6	4	6	4	6	4	5
5	9	5	9	5	7	5	7	5	7	5	7	5	6	5	7	5	7	5	7	5	7	5	6
6	10	6	10	6	8	6	8	6	8	6	8	6	7	6	8	6	8	6	8	6	8	6	7
7	11	7	11	7	9	7	9	7	9	7	9	7	8	7	9	7	9	7	9	7	9	7	8
8	12	8	12	8	10	8	10	8	10	8	10	8	9	8	10	8	10	8	10	8	10	8	9
9	13	9	13	9	11	9	11	9	11	9	11	9	10	9	11	9	11	9	11	9	11	9	10
10	14	10	14	10	12	10	12	10	12	10	12	10	11	10	12	10	12	10	12	10	12	10	11
11	15	11	15	11	13	11	13	11	13	11	13	11	12	11	13	11	13	11	13	11	13	11	12
12	16	12	16	12	14	12	14	12	14	12	14	12	13	12	14	12	14	12	14	12	14	12	13
13	17	13	17	13	15	13	15	13	15	13	15	13	14	13	15	13	15	13	15	13	15	13	14
14	18	14	18	14	16	14	16	14	16	14	16	14	15	14	16	14	16	14	16	14	16	14	15
15	19	15	19	15	17	15	17	15	17	15	17	15	16	15	17	15	17	15	17	15	17	15	16
16	20	16	20	16	18	16	18	16	18	16	18	16	17	16	18	16	18	16	18	16	18	16	17
17	21	17	21	17	19	17	19	17	19	17	19	17	18	17	19	17	19	17	19	17	19	17	18
18	22	18	22	18	20	18	20	18	20	18	20	18	19	18	20	18	20	18	20	18	20	18	19
19	23	19	23	19	21	19	21	19	21	19	21	19	20	19	21	19	21	19	21	19	21	19	20
20	24	20	24	20	22	20	22	20	22	20	22	20	21	20	22	20	22	20	22	20	22	20	21
21	25	21	25	21	23	21	23	21	23	21	23	21	22	21	23	21	23	21	23	21	23	21	22
22	26	22	26	22	24	22	24	22	24	22	24	22	23	22	24	22	24	22	24	22	24	22	23
23	27	23	27	23	25	23	25	23	25	23	25	23	24	23	25	23	25	23	25	23	25	23	24
24	28	24	28	24	26	24	26	24	26	24	26	24	25	24	26	24	26	24	26	24	26	24	25
25	29	25	29	25	27	25	27	25	27	25	27	25	26	25	27	25	27	25	27	25	27	25	26
26	30	26	30	26	28	26	28	26	28	26	28	26	27	26	28	26	28	26	28	26	28	26	27
27	31	27	1 (MAY)	27	29	27	29	27	29	27	29	27	28	27	29	27	29	27	29	27	29	27	28
28	1 (APRIL)	28	2	28	30	28	30	28	30	28	30	28	29	28	30	28	30	28	30	28	30	28	1 (MAR.)
29	2	29	3	29	31	29	1 (JULY)	29	31	29	31	29	30	29	31	29	1 (DEC)	29	31	29	31	29	2
30	3			30	1 (JUNE)	30	2	30	1 (AUG)	30	1 (SEP.)	30	1 (OCT)	30	1 (NOV)	30	2	30	1 (JAN.)	30	1 (FEB.)	30	3
31	4			31	2			31	2			31	2	31	2			31	2			31	4

be purchased in tablet form at any chemist. Ask for Calcium *with* Vitamin **D.** The diet should be varied – raw or cooked meat, rabbit, heart, liver (cooked), fish, whale-meat, etc. If herrings are given, brown bread or some cereal should be given as this fish is very rich.

Milk, if given, should be regarded as an extra food, and remember never, at any age in a cat's life, give milk and raw meat together. At least one hour should elapse between.

Never, at any time, lift a cat by its neck without giving support to the hind quarters. Would you like to feel the weight of your body by being picked up by the neck? Of course you would not! so why should your cat? In a pregnant queen this may even cause injury.

Your queen will probably investigate every cupboard, open drawer or box she can find, trying to decide where to have her kittens, but if, from time to time, during her pregnancy, especially the last week, you put her in her maternity box, in all probability she will finally settle there.

There is something inexplicably exciting, thrilling and intriguing in one's first litter of kittens, and although more years have passed over my head than I care to think about since my first queen was delivered of her first litter, I still have that thrill on the arrival of each litter, which nothing else can give.

Birth of Kittens

Many people think there is something exceptional about a kitten being born feet first. Discussions with Veterinary Surgeons and other breeders show that 50 per cent of kittens are born this way.

Do not develop a complex that Siamese are difficult in giving birth to their kittens, or that they must have this, that and the other. Siamese Cats are not the delicate creatures some folk would have you believe. Unless there is need to help her, your queen is best left alone during kittening. Some queens demand their owner to stay with them, or sometimes another animal friend.

Difficulties can be caused by a dead kitten obstructing the fallopian tube, or a breach birth. If the queen has laboured for some hours without producing a kitten, send for the vet. When all the kittens are born, the little mother will settle down. Prepare a thick layer of paper and a warm blanket folded to size of box,

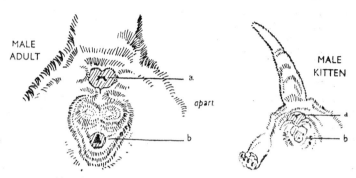

*Note that study of mature animals will perfect knowledge
of slight development in kittens.*

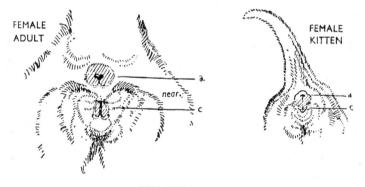

SEX DIAGRAM

*The ability to tell the sex of kittens is easily acquired by reference to the diagram
and the application of factual knowledge of the sex organs. Allowance should be
made in size between the adult cat and kittens, but the principle is the same.*

*In the upper half of the diagram, 'a' indicates the anus, and 'b' the sheath covering
the male organ. Directly behind 'b' is the scrotum which fills out as development
takes place. In the lower half, 'a' again indicates the anus and 'c' the entrance to
the female organ. This leaflet can be obtained from the Cats' Protection League.*

Courtesy of the Cats' Protection League

lift the queen and kittens on to the blanket, remove the torn paper from the box, then lift the prepared bed, paper, blanket and kittens back into the box. The family will then be warm and comfortable. This may seem quite an operation, but it is all done in a minute if properly undertaken. Take care the room is not draughty.

Do NOT try to sex them. If you want boys and they are girls, you cannot change them, so why bother? Give the mother a drink of glucose and milk, or egg and milk if possible, and allow them quiet and rest. Some queens are so attentive to their offspring that they do not leave the nest to pass water. See that she does this within a reasonable period. Barley water is a help, and with glucose added, most queens will take it readily.

Should you have to help a queen it is, as with most things in life, a matter of common sense! If you have actually to deliver the kittens, see that you get the afterbirth. Each kitten is born in a sac complete with afterbirth, or placenta. The cord has to be severed and can be cut with scissors (have scissors boiled and sterilized), or severed with the thumb and finger (hands disinfected). This is the method I was shown, but have found scissors quite satisfactory, the main point being that the cord must not be cut too near the kitten's body. In taking the afterbirth from the queen, the cord must be firmly held between the thumb and finger of the left hand about two inches from the kitten's body, for if the cord is pulled roughly from this side, the kitten may have an umbilical hernia, which may not be serious but is unnecessary. With the thumb and finger of the right hand withdraw the placenta or afterbirth, moving the finger forward as it is drawn out, so that the strain does not break the cord. I would advise using thumb and finger for your first effort – you can then weigh up for yourself if you are competent to use the more direct method. Take care to sterilize your hands, and everything you use.

It does sometimes happen that kittens arrive too quickly for the queen to give prompt attention to each one. If you have to deal with the kittens, wipe the mucus from their mouths and nostrils and dry with a towel, for it is the action of the mother's rough tongue that stimulates the kitten, and you are for the moment taking her place. If a kitten appears to be stuck, it is worrying, but do not panic or you will convey this agitation to your queen. Collect cotton wool and towels, well wash the hands, taking care to scrub finger nails, wrap cotton wool or towel (you must decide this for yourself) round the protruding portion of the kitten, and each time the queen strains EASE the kitten. DO NOT PULL, for you will readily understand that a kitten does not stretch. You MUST ease the whole body.

A breeder wrote me once, explaining how she had used olive oil when her queen had been in labour for many hours and then just a tail appeared. She filled a clinical pipette with the oil and easing it gently past the tail, released the oil. The kitten was born within seconds. Do not be put off by the word 'clinical'. All you want to ascertain is that the end of the pipette which enters the body is smooth and round, not just a sharp edge.

It is most unwise to hold a tail thus appearing too firmly, especially in Siamese, whose tails taper to a fine point, but it is always easy to be wise after the event.

Sometimes maiden queens have difficulty with their first litter. The young mother is bewildered by the arrival of the first kitten. I recall one who was most difficult with her first litter and had to be helped with each one. Fearing the worst when the next litter was due, preparations were made for all contingencies and the vet warned. She was five days late and then, owing to unavoidable circumstances, had to be left for three-and-a-half hours. In that time she produced six kittens all by herself. They were not all quite dry, but were clean and tidy. Mama, with a look of smug satisfaction and pride, seemed to say: 'What on earth you made all the fuss and bother about, I fail to understand . . . Humans! Ab-solute-ly unpredictable!!!'

By the way, if you use rubber gloves, see that they have been sterilized, and use the surgical type.

Should a kitten appear to be dead, never take it for granted. Place it on a warm blanket. The blanket should be torn in pieces to make a nest – this is much warmer than one piece – and lie on the hot water tank or some such continuous and steady heat; the top cover of an Aga Cooker is excellent. If you use hot water bottles they should be replaced frequently in order to maintain the temperature necessary.

Warmth and their mother's milk and quiet are all kittens need for a while.

Should a queen lose all her kittens, and have a great deal of milk, it should clear without difficulty. A *little* Epsom Salts in the food will help. Should it not clear, consult your vet. The modern treatment is tablets of Strobestrol or Diencestrol.

Should your queen 'call' again soon after her losing her kittens, do not mate her until the next 'call'.

Again, if your queen 'calls' while nursing her kittens, it is not always wise to keep her 'back' too long. I once had a queen who after years of 'calling' at reasonable intervals, called 5 days after the birth of her kittens – for 3 days – and then again at 10 to 14 day intervals. In this way she had called quite a few times before being mated again. This happened twice; on both occasions she produced in the litter one or two dead, and a not so normal birth, or both.

My veterinary Surgeon and I discussed the matter and thought the constant calling had a bad effect, and decided to mate her on her second call provided it was at least three weeks after the birth of the litter, the resulting kittens to be weaned early.

This had the desired effect – she returned to normal, producing the litter without difficulty and all alive.

Do not overhandle your litter when they are in the nest, but handle sufficiently for them to know the human smell so that they are not nervous kittens.

A nursing queen needs MORE CALCIUM while feeding her family than during the period of gestation.

Although I give Robinson's Groats with Froment or Bemax and Glucose morning and evening, I do not agree with the theory that queens should have only milk foods for two or three days after the birth of the kittens – in fact I give raw, lean meat on the first day. Vary the diet as much as possible; do not give a mixture of Vitamins unless your queen needs them. Bemax, Froment and Kit-zymes are excellent in fulfilling the need for Vitamin B. Kit-zymes are in tablet form and most cats will come running at the rattle of the tin.

If your queen has a miscarriage before the full period, there must be some cause, usually one of the following:

Insufficient Vitamin E;
an unhealthy condition of the uterus;
a fall while jumping too great a height.

The first can be remedied by daily tablets of Ephynol or Wheat Germ Oil in capsule form, which should be given during the pregnancy. The second is outside your province – consult your vet. Should your queen continually 'miss', when mated, give a course of Vitamin E (Ephynol) and Halibut Oil. It may be an acid condition which destroys the sperms before they can be fertilized, in which case your vet can help.

Hormones can be given, you must decide for yourselves in this matter – personally I do not feel that sufficient is known about their reaction in any given animal. A hormone that suits one cat will not suit another. Cases have been known when females so treated have become masculine and spayed permanently in the manner of a male – losing all femininity. If your queen mis-mates, an injection of Stiboestrol is given; this stops the unwanted litter, but often upsets the balance of nature and the following 'call' and mating is unfruitful.

I should like to dispose of the myths (1) that this injection stops a queen ever having kittens again and (2) that a queen mis-mated with black, tabby or any other colour or breed of cat, is spoilt for breeding pedigree kittens. Let us look at this myth logically. The kitten is the result of the mating of two cats; once the kittens are born, the queen returns to normal. Any subsequent mating with a pure pedigree will produce pure bred kittens. However, should your queen mis-mate do watch carefully and on no account overlook giving her olive oil or medicated paraffin for the last week of pregnancy – for the heads of mongrel litters will probably be larger than those of Siamese kittens.

False Pregnancy

This is an unexplained phenomenon. The queen goes the full period of gestation, will increase in size, look for a nest to have her kittens, tearing up paper, etc., even to having milk and then – NO kittens, and she returns to normal size.

You may want your queen to foster another kitten. Do not put directly to the breast. Smear with a little butter and place the kitten so that it crawls to her breast between her hind legs. This will help to remove any strange smell the kitten may have. Your queen will, in cleaning it up, accept it as one of her own.

Finally I must mention two difficulties you may encounter, although they are not common occurrences.

1. The queen's milk being acid may upset the kittens and can cause death, but please do not panic at these words. The remedy is very simple. To be on the safe side give a pinch of citrate of soda for at least a week before the birth of the kittens, and carry on through the nursing period. If tablets are given, they can be given whole or dissolved in milk or water.

2. Kittens fading out at four to six weeks, and gummy eyes in kittens. By 'fading' kittens, I mean those that just seem to fade away. This may be all bound up with abortions, open eye kittens and so on. The cause is so far unknown, and therefore the treatment is unknown. Success has been claimed for giving penicillin half-way through the pregnancy but it does not always work. Veterinary surgeons have been working on this for years.

Following the birth of kittens, queens sometimes discharge blood or blood-stained fluid. It is impossible to give specific advice on this, for a certain amount of discharge often follows the birth. Keep the part bathed with T.C.P. Should it be persistent, or the smallest amount of pus appear, consult your vet.

Caesarean Births

Modern surgery has made this commonplace. Some people think this affects a queen for further breeding. This is not so – neither does it mean that her next litter will not arrive normally. I have personal knowledge of queens who have not needed a second caesarean. Do not be alarmed if your queen has to have this operation; she will feed her kittens and carry on normally.

CHAPTER SEVEN

Kitten Rearing

THE REARING OF KITTENS requires common sense and understanding. Before undertaking the responsibility make sure you understand what it entails. A little time spent in studying other people's experiences will save a lot of worry when the time comes for the great adventure.

Draughts are bad for young kittens. Whilst it is important to keep kittens warm, do not use feather pillows; they are too heating and tend to create a desire for extra warmth in the bodies of young kittens. All Siamese kittens are born pure white. One could not by any stretch of imagination call them beautiful, but they have a fascination, even at this age, and as they develop, and their points begin to appear on the tips of the ears, nose, paws and tail, they are not only attractive but intriguing. Normally the points start to develop about the eighth or ninth day.

Kittens will cry if they are not getting enough food. Make certain the mother's milk is coming through. If all breasts are not functioning, bathe with warm water and press from the side until the milk flows. Very rarely one gets a blind breast. This is a job for the vet.

Kittens seem to open their eyes earlier and earlier and it is now quite usual for the eyes to be open at five days. They should not be exposed to bright light for a week or so, and while on the subject of brightness, kittens should not at any time be left in the sunlight without the opportunity to move into the shade.

If any one kitten has his eyes gummed up, it should be bathed once, with boracic lotion. If persistent, there are many modern eye ointments obtainable from your chemist or vet.

Should you have to feed the kittens from birth, I find a hypodermic syringe or pipette excellent. The plunger of the syringe can be pressed so slightly that the kitten draws as if from the breast.

The first feeds should be glucose and boiled water, following on with Lactol or the baby food you prefer. Even when kittens are feeding from their mother, it is wise, with a litter of four or more to help your queen by giving the kittens a little Lactol or baby food, mixed to a consistency that the kittens will take readily. Some kittens are very slow to lap. Encourage them, by offering milky food on your finger. They will usually lick this. Move the finger nearer and nearer to the saucer, until it is nearly submerged in the food. The kitten, in licking your finger, will find himself lapping.

The chief ingredients in rearing healthy kittens are sunlight, fresh air, warmth, sleep, exercise, cleanliness, regular meals and common sense.

Feed kittens separately with their main meals; not only do you know they have the amount required for their growth and well-being, but with larger kittens there is the inclination to rush their food, to get as much as possible before the others.

Should you want to mark your kittens for any reason, i.e., one selected by a purchaser – or any other reason – the best method is gentian violet, under or between the front paws. In my early days, I marked two kittens of a litter with lipstick! How optimistic one can be? Mama either did not like the decoration or maybe she disliked the taste. Whatever the reason, she soon removed it!

Kittens are trained by their mother in house manners as soon as they run about, and it is very interesting to see the mother discipline a youngster that is inclined to be naughty. It is important that toilet trays are provided large enough to accommodate all the kittens of a litter and the trays must be changed at least once a day and, as the kittens grow, twice a day. Kittens always look for the tray in the same place, and it is therefore important not to move it about; for young kittens paper torn up into small pieces can be used, as they grow older, introduce peat moss or one of the many products now on the market for this special purpose. Don't throw it away when used. Put it on the compost heap. It hastens the decomposition of vegetable matter and is turned into excellent compost.

Like most young things, kittens need lots of sleep in their early months and it is essential that they are not unduly disturbed. Warmth and food are of course also important. To ensure proper development, food should be given at regular intervals.

At first the diet should be light – plaice or fresh haddock. The coarser fish, although suitable for older cats, should not be given to young kittens. Herrings are risky, although their vitamin content is great.

The diet should be varied as the kittens grow. Steamed plaice, later haddock, rabbit, raw and cooked lean meat. Remove all bones from cooked rabbit and fish before feeding.

At fourteen days or so the kittens will become more active and at three weeks it is wise – even essential with a litter of five or more – to relieve the strain on the queen by giving the kittens Lactol, or one of the recognized baby foods. Personally, I find Lactol ideal as it is easily mixed and specially prepared for young animals. Fed with a pipette or hypodermic syringe; the kittens will soon learn to take the food this way.

At a month to five weeks they will probably show interest in their mother's food. It is time then to introduce fish in the form of steamed plaice. At six weeks raw scraped meat can be givens There has always been a difference of opinion amongst breeder. as to the best age to feed raw meat. Experience shows that kittens invariably make forward strides once raw *scraped* meat is introduced to their diet. But do not overdo this – and the meat *must* be scraped.

Large meals do not necessarily promote growth. If overfed, kittens will have upset digestions and this can mean setbacks. From Lactol, progress to Robinson's Groats or Farex, add a little glucose. For kittens that are backward, there are a number of modern remedies. Amongst the best are Abedex and Radiostol.

Once weaned, kittens need four meals a day at least, until six months. Three meals should be given until twelve months, then two. The right amount of food for a three months old kitten is a good tablespoonful. Water should be at hand at all times and it should be fresh each day.

With your first litter there is always the temptation to handle them. Resist it! See that all is well and leave them. All they need for a while is their mother's milk and sleep. Don't be too anxious to know the sex. If you want females and they are males, you cannot alter the sex, so be patient.

It is a wonderful sight to see kittens, having played until they are tired, come to their mother and one by one settle down for.

a drink, all cuddled near her – and then mother and kittens fast asleep, the kittens heaped on top of one another.

Kittens born with their eyes open should not be kept. If they survive they may not be good breeders and there is the possibility of their even passing this congenital fault to their children.

FEEDING CHART FOR KITTENS
AT SIX WEEKS AND UPWARD

7.30 – 8.0 a.m.
Fish cooked in milk (I start my kittens on plaice).
Mid-morning:
Top of the milk cream. Cow & Gate or any of the similar baby foods.
12.30 – 1.0 p.m.
Finely cut rabbit, raw beef or horse flesh (remember bicarbonate).
5.0 – 6.0 p.m.
Cooked rabbit, meat or fish.

As kittens grow the size of meals should be increased and the intervals between meals extended.

Just before going to bed give a little groats to content the kittens for the night. This – as the mid-day feed – should not be large.

A drop of Halibut Oil daily is excellent and a little Calcium Lactate (can be purchased in powder form or tablets). Kit-zyme tablets daily for periods, not continuously. Each meal of solid food should be roughly 1 to $1\frac{1}{2}$ tablespoonful. Always give kittens access to fresh water.

One receives many interesting and amusing letters through one's kittens and often lasting friendships result. Mrs. Nancy Fellows' letter expresses so well what the arrival of her Siamese kitten meant to her and her family that I feel it's only proper that it should be included in this book.

Who, if they haven't experienced this kind of enchantment, can understand that a whole hour passes in ten minutes with a piece of string and a swan's feather; or that even the dreariest of household chores has become an uproarious sort of game, and that everything takes twice the time that it used to?

Who would expect that this little fur-clad creature could

contain so much insight and resourcefulness, so much affection and concern, such caution and utter recklessness? That he can tumble into calamity with the cheerful humility of a circus clown, resemble a mischievous imp with a dirty face, or suggest the lovely relief border on a Jasper vase, all in the same breath?

When I see those long, long tinted arms hanging down into space from widespread elbows irregularly bent; head thrust forward and a 'What-shall-we-do-next, I'm willing' expression in his eyes – then time stops, and I am utterly and hopelessly lost . . .

Well, he grows larger and silkier, louder of purr and even more beautiful, and knows everything even when he's asleep. (I think he's psychic!) He eats and enjoys all the meals you prescribe, is magnificently fit, and only has one phobia so far. That is the B.B.C. chimes of 'Big Ben', which he simply cannot endure! At the second stroke he trembles from nose to tail, flattens himself on the floor, crawls to the door and dashes madly upstairs to the top shelf of the airing cupboard, there to remain till it's all safely over. However, a little forethought and the switch of a knob is no difficulty . .

He has an endearing way of sharing his charms and attentions in the family, so that we all feel important for different reasons, while his faithfulness is frightening!

Yes, there must be volumes of space for unwritten phrases and unheard praises.

CHAPTER EIGHT

The Stud Cat

HAVING KEPT STUD CATS for many years, I strongly advise those of you thinking of keeping a stud, not to make up your mind until you have weighed up the pros and cons. The work entails much responsibility, time and patience. Visiting queens are often nervous and difficult – and if one is to be successful there must be complete confidence and understanding between the Stud and his owner. The Stud must be allowed freedom when mating a queen and not be interfered with by its owner. Otherwise he will lose confidence and become nervous; this nervousness in turn can be conveyed to the queen. The Stud should only mate a queen when under observation. If the Stud and queen are allowed to run loose, one cannot be sure that the mating has taken place, on the other hand both could mate until they reach the stage of exhaustion. One has a responsibility to the owner of the queen and to one's own Stud.

If you are nervous or highly strung, do not undertake stud work; it is interesting and exacting, at times needing much patience.

Stud cats are not fierce; most are the gentlest of creatures and very affectionate. They will however protect themselves if attacked by another tom. NEVER attempt to pick up your cat, male or female, if in a fight. In the heat of the moment you may be bitten, for their minds are on their enemy. The circumstances must decide your method of stopping the fight. Maybe a good 'Shoo! Shoo!' will send off the visitor; but, if in real combat, words are useless. A wire fire-screen, piece of wood, anything solid, can be eased between the contestants, or a rug dropped over one's own pet. Don't rush in – it will be QUICKER AND SAFER to think before you take action.

A full male, on attaining maturity, will usually spray (instead of using his toilet tray); he will spray on curtains, loose covers and furniture, and your home will not be free of the smell of tom cat – not very pleasant for your household or your friends!

I do *not* recommend keeping a Stud cat indoors for I think they function much better when housed out of doors, where they have plenty of fresh air and exercise. When housed out of doors, the stud house need not be large, but it must be large enough to accommodate a reasonable-sized pen for the visiting queen and, to give the Stud ample freedom of movement, a wired-in run as large as possible should be provided, with free access from the stud house.

The house should be furnished with shelves – one under the window enabling him to look out – and at least one other, also a stool or chair. Lino on the floor makes cleaning easier, but, as it does not give a grip, I find it more convenient to put a piece of carpet, or small rug down, thus enabling the Stud and queen to get a foothold. Location is important. The house and run should be so placed that it is within view of the owner's house. The Stud can then catch every movement.

Although I have known of two Stud cats who lived together, generally this is not advisable. It is wise to have a separate house and run for each Stud.

Heating. If the stud house is built of wood, it is advisable to have it lined; this can be done with hardboard or one of the various woods that are on the market today – if necessary the space between outside wall and lining wood can be filled with glass fibre, or other insulating material.

If you are going to use oil heating, see that there is no chance of the stove being knocked over. Have a wire guard made to go over the stove, the top of which can be of asbestos; the heat then radiates out and the asbestos top forms a warm seat for your Stud. Any form of oil lamp heating should hang on a swivel hook. The late Miss F. Dixon, Hon. Treasurer of the Siamese Cat Club for many years, used this form of heating.

Infra-red Dull Emitter appliances are used with great success. Dr. and Mrs. Francis of Low Knap, Devon, tell me they find 'Laybat' the most effective. These Dull Emitters are economical and longer-lasting than the glass lamp and, even more important, the Dull Emitter allows complete rest at night, there being no bright light.

Mrs. D. Barnes wrote me of a heater she uses: 'There are two makes, the "Eltex" and the "Swift" and my husband has drawn a rough diagram for you to see [*see below*]. The bulb is made of some hard substance and looks something like stone and is surrounded with a heavy metal guard. The beauty of it is that, owing to the thermostat, you can set it at any temperature you wish and once it reaches that figure, it automatically switches itself off'.

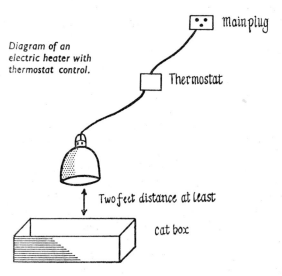

Diagram of an electric heater with thermostat control.

Main plug

Thermostat

Two feet distance at least

cat box

I have replaced my oil heating with tubular heating in the stud houses. If tubular heaters are used, a shelf should be fixed above the heater to stop the Stud touching it and it also forms a warm place for him to sit.

From time to time one reads comments on Stud Cats leading lonely lives. Although Studs live alone they are not lonely – they do not miss a single movement of wind, falling leaves, passing 'planes and even the moving clouds interest them. I do not agree with Studs being kept in stud houses without access to any outside run for exercise and fresh air. To my mind, for healthy body and mind (yes, I mean 'mind'; it is not a slip of my pen), a Stud cat must have air, exercise and good food.

Never put two queens in the Stud's house at the same time – they will probably be upset by each other's scent even if in different pens; and it is not fair to divide the male's attention.

Siamese males often come to sexual maturity quite early, but it is not advisable to use at stud too soon. If it is necessary he could be used at nine months, but a year is better.

When a queen visits a Stud, it is usual to mate her twice, within twenty-four hours. The stud fee covers one visit only. Should no offspring result from these matings, another mating is usually given free, on the queen's next call, but this is not compulsory – it is a courtesy on the part of the stud owner.

The stud fee should be paid before the queen is returned to the owner.

Owners of Queens: It is most important that you notify the owner of the Stud you intend to use, when the queen starts 'calling'. It is most embarrassing to have a 'calling' queen with owner arrive at one's house, without notice. What is to be done if there is already a queen with the Stud she wishes to use? Well, generally speaking, owners of Studs and 'calling' queens are reasonable and some solution is found, but do telephone the day your queen starts to call and arrange for her to visit the Stud of your choice. Personally I think the third day of call is the best day to take a queen, but should no offspring result from this mating, try a later day on the second attempt.

Owners of queens should be careful to mention any odd habits of their queen, so that the stud owner is warned. Another DO – take your queen to the stud in a basket; it is much safer than just carrying her.

The usual method is to put the 'calling' queen in a pen within the Stud's house; thus they make each other's acquaintance through the wire. When the queen settles down and becomes used to the presence of her intended mate, when they croon to one another, this is the moment to let her out. After mating most queens turn on the Stud – not viciously (although some can be vicious) and the Stud jumps away – the queen will roll in varied degrees of ecstasy, often pushing herself along the ground. I have known them rush madly round the stud house. Do not attempt to put her in her pen until she is quiet – if she spits and puts her claws out at you, it is your own fault, but more important, it interrupts the physical reaction of the mating, which is unfair to the queen.

If your queen has a tendency to be spiteful when 'calling',

tell the stud owner who will be prepared. It must be remembered that this is a time of high emotion in the queen's life, when they are often difficult.

Although a queen is normally quite good at home, some of them can be very difficult when they meet their Stud. It is a good idea for stud houses to have a portion lined with zinc for its toilet tray. It is important that the tray and drinking water should be changed daily. A deep box made of wood, or a small barrel on its side, should be provided for the Stud's winter sleeping quarters. Queens should not be brought to stud on a lead or in too small a basket. They should be made quite comfortable in their own basket of reasonable size, otherwise they can become frightened and upset.

Stud cats must be well-fed. They should have two good meals a day all the year round and during the season when queens are numerous this should be increased to three meals a day. The main diet of my Studs is raw meat. This I vary with rabbit, hare, whale-meat, fish, stew, etc. I also give Vitamins from time to time, and Cod Liver Oil and Ribena in winter months. Barley should also be included in the diet as this is helpful to the kidneys. Clean fresh water should always be available, as Studs drink a great deal, especially during the mating season.

Studs exercise by playing and climbing in their runs, but should be allowed the run of the garden, under supervision. When he is sniffing about, do not touch him, or pick him up suddenly. If he has been smelling another tom cat's spirt, it is possible he will jump and bite without warning, thinking whatever touches him (in this case your hand) is the male he is at the moment smelling.

After a queen has visited your Stud, it is important that the pen she has used is cleaned and disinfected. For general disinfecting I have used Cromessol with much satisfaction for many years. The base is formaldehyde. It has a pleasant smell and is clean to use. It is made by The Cremossol Company Limited, Glasgow. Sprays of different sizes can also be obtained from the same firm.

CHAPTER NINE

Neuters

NEUTERED SIAMESE have been popular for some years. The neutering operation does not affect their character, or intelligence, in any way – in fact many people think they become even more affectionate after neutering. If you do not intend to breed, it is much more convenient to have your kitten neutered. This is best done between the age of three and five months. If it is delayed beyond six months the Law provides that an anaesthetic must be given to prevent the animal feeling any pain.

The neutering of male cats is known as castrating and that of females as spaying. When un-neutered males reach the age of maturity, they naturally desire a mate and if allowed free range may wander to find one, perhaps getting into fights in the process. At this stage they may spray indoors, which is most unpleasant as their urine is strong-smelling. The spaying of females has been brought to such a high pitch of perfection that the operation is no longer considered to be dangerous and kittens can now be spayed at the early age of eleven weeks.

The spaying of an adult Siamese is a major operation and should not be performed when the queen is 'calling'. Although there is always a risk when an anaesthetic has to be given, the advancement of Veterinary Science has reduced all risks to a minimum and in these days both male and female adults can be neutered without difficulty.

The general tendency with owners of neuters is to over-feed them – although this is done in kindness, it is not good – if your Siamese neuter becomes too fat, he will probably become lethargic and this in turn may lead to illness. Out of mistaken kindness many folk feed their neuter friend at every meal, and in between! As he is not hunting for his food or reproducing himself, the food does not produce extra energy, but extra fat – which in turn makes him less inclined to take exercise. Yes, I realise there is a special reason why you, my reader, with a huge neutered Siamese, have to feed yours so much! We all deceive ourselves into believing what we want to believe and I know you do it out of mistaken kindness, but don't overtax his digestive powers, or allow him to run to solid fat.

For many years there has been much speculation as to which sex makes the best pet. Personally I don't think there is any difference. To achieve the perfect solution if possible have one of each, for then you will find that they have great games together and this gives them plenty of exercise.

Breeders are often asked to have a kitten neutered or spayed before it goes to its new owner. In the male kitten the testicles have to descend from the abdomen; this happens at about three to four months, so that neutering cannot be done until that time. Some people feel that a male should be allowed further development, say to nine months and then be neutered; others that a male should not be neutered until he has attained manhood and mated a few queens. It is a matter for personal choice.

Again in the spaying of females there are two schools of thought:

(1) that this should be done as early as ten weeks, which means that the organ of fertility is removed, and does not therefore grow;

(2) that the queen should be allowed to have one litter, that is allow the reproductive organs to mature. After the birth of the kittens and the physical condition returns to normal, the operation of spaying is then performed.

To be happy and healthy all Siamese need exercise. If your cat cannot have free range, then I did mention earlier a harness and lead. They are soft and close-fitting without pressure; they are safe and strong. I can recommend them. The harness is braid elastic covered with rayon or nylon, so causing no rub. The set, which can be purchased in various colours, consists of brace, lead and collar – each separate. My objection to leather harness is the rub it may cause.

Special Classes are provided for Neuters at all Cat Shows.

CHAPTER TEN

The Governing Council of the Cat Fancy

THE ORGANISATION which regulates the affairs of the Cat Fancy is the Governing Council of the Cat Fancy, which came into being on March 8th, 1910. Prior to its formation two separate bodies, The National Cat Club and The Cat Club, registered cats and framed their own rules for exhibition of Cats and Kittens. Thus the Cat Fancy was divided into two separate groups; this division caused much confusion and difficulty, and although many attempts were made to settle their problems, it was not until March 8th, 1910, that agreement was reached. The functions of the new body were to draw up a set of rules for the exhibition and showing of cats, to act as a central authority and Court of Appeal in all matters relating to cats and to arrange for the registration of all breeds of Cats and Kittens.

The fundamental objective of the Council at its formation was to provide a system where all exhibitors at Cat Shows would have the same opportunity and the exhibits could be judged solely on their merits. The only method which would satisfy this objective and provide a means of identifying each Cat or Kitten under distinctive names and with an identity number was the introduction of a Register in which all the necessary particulars were recorded.

The Council consists of properly elected delegates from affiliated Cat Clubs and Societies, whether Specialist or All-Breed Clubs. Election of delegates is held annually before 15th March each year. Each Club elects its delegate or delegates either by postal ballot or at its Annual Meeting. Each delegate holds office for one year commencing 1st April but is eligible for re-election. New Clubs as they affiliate can apply for representation when they have fifty paid-up members.

The Council elects its own Chairman, Officers and Executive Committee. Ordinary meetings are held in July, October and February, the Annual Meeting is in April and the Executive

Committee meets as and when required. The Council is financed by the subscriptions of its members and by the fees charged for its various services.

Each breed has a separate identity number. The breed numbers for Siamese are:

Seal Pointed	...	...	Breed Number 24
Blue Pointed	...	...	Breed Number 24a
Chocolate Pointed		...	Breed Number 24b
Lilac Pointed	...	...	Breed Number 24c

For the payment of a moderate fee a breeder can purchase the right to the exclusive use of a distinguishing 'Prefix' for the stock he or she breeds. The Council employ a Secretary and Assistant Secretary, who are responsible for the registration of all cats and kittens. The time and labour employed in the work is considerable and for this service a small fee is charged for each entry in the Register.

Registration. It is not necessary to register all the kittens one breeds. However, it should be remembered that if one takes out a 'Prefix' or Cattery name, kittens bred at the Cattery can be recognized at once by having a distinguishing name. On the other hand, all the kittens one breeds do not measure up to the required standard and one is not bound to register all the stock one breeds. Having made that clear, here are the details required for registering a kitten.

Application to register a kitten must be made on the official form – 'Application for Registration' – issued by the Governing Council of the Cat Fancy. The information required is the breed number, colour, sex, name of the kitten and the date of birth, also name and address of breeder, the name of the sire, its registered number, breed number and name of owner. Similar information is also required regarding the dam; the names of both grand-parents in each case must also be given. On receipt of the completed form and provided the breeder has complied with the regulations regarding the name of the kitten, the Council will issue a registration certificate. This records the official number allotted to the kitten, together with its official name. The certificate is in fact a birth certificate on which is recorded all the appropriate details. When a registered kitten is sold, it must be officially transferred to its new owner. It is important to remember that, until it is officially transferred to its new owner on the official transfer form, the kitten remains registered in the name of the breeder.

CHAPTER ELEVEN

Exhibiting and Cat Shows

IT'S A FAR CRY to the year 1871 in which the first Cat Show was held in Britain, yet at that time the Show held at the Crystal Palace attracted a large number of exhibits. There are three types of Cat Shows: Championship Cat Shows at which Challenge Certificates issued by the Governing Council of the Cat Fancy are awarded in the Open Breed Classes – a cat winning three Challenge Certificates under different Judges at three different Shows is awarded the G.C.C.F. Championship and becomes a full Champion. Sanction Shows are Shows which do not carry the Championship status. Exemption Shows – a show at which Pedigree Cats registered with the G.C.C.F. can be shown even if the Show is not held under G.C.C.F. Rules. With the exception of Kittens in Litter Classes and Neuters, every Cat or Kitten exhibited at a Show held under G.C.C.F. Rules, must, previous to the date of the Show, have been entered in the Register kept for that purpose alone. The particulars required to be recorded are the name, the date of birth, name of sire and dam, and of grandsire and granddam. If the age, pedigree or breeder's name is not known, the cat or kitten must be registered as age, breeder or pedigree not known. Where there is a change of ownership the transfer of the Cat or Kitten must be registered with the G.C.C.F. and no cat or kitten will be eligible for exhibition at any show until the registration has been made. Since 1950 Premier Certificates for Neuters only are awarded at Championship Shows, to be eligible for competition in these Classes. Neuters also must be registered with the G.C.C.F.

Championship Shows are held in London from July to January, and in the Provinces from September to February. Sanction and Exemption Shows are held in the provinces all the year round. A list of Shows licensed by the G.C.C.F. is available about May each year and can be obtained post free from the Secretary; application for Show Schedules should be made to the Show

Manager whose name will be shown on the list.

The Rules for all Championship Shows are in principle the same. It is important to study the Rules carefully because, to ensure fair competition, they are strictly observed. The main points are – each exhibit on arrival is examined by the Club's Honorary Veterinary Surgeons and any cats which are unfit for exhibition will be removed from the Show Hall. All exhibits must be in suitable boxes or baskets, have clean ears and be free from vermin. No interior or exterior decorations or distinguishing objects, such as coloured blankets, are allowed in or on the pens. White blankets only and suitable sanitary tins must be provided by the exhibitor. When completing entry forms it is well to remember that, if the particulars shown do not correspond with the registration, Prize Money could be forfeited. Tallies are issued to exhibitors before the Show; these correspond with the pen number and must be tied round the exhibit's neck with white tape. Before prize winners can be paid out, each entry is checked by the G.C.C.F. to ensure that it agrees with the Register. This is an important safeguard to ensure the identity of each exhibit.

The general everyday preparation for exhibiting is fresh air and grooming, good feeding, good housing and as much freedom as is consistent with safety. Those are the basic essentials for your cat being in the best possible condition on Show Day. Brushing is explained in Chapter Four.

If your cat is at all nervous, purchase a wire pen and place your cat in this for a few minutes each day, lengthening the time until he has occupied the pen for the full Show period. An exhibitor who shows a cat which is likely to be bad tempered is not only risking the well-being of his cat, but also an attack on the Judge or Steward and the upsetting of other exhibits. Cats that cannot be handled by Stewards are disqualified.

Lilli Palmer, star of Bell, Book and Candle, *is seen here with Pyewacket (and understudy). Both cats were bred by the Author.*

When Miss Joan Greenwood (left) took over the role of Gillian Holroyd in the play, Pyewacket warmly welcomed his new leading lady with a Siamese's customary hospitality.

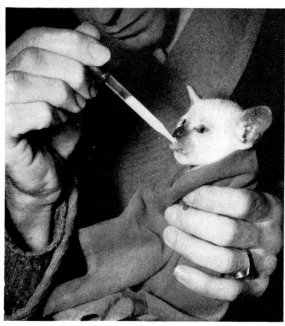

Timshel Titian Tarrago, at 4 weeks lapped free and greedily. A gre drinker he was nam after a Greek god and Spanish wine. Bred Mrs. H. N. Lovemore.

The author with two of her cats.

CHAPTER TWELVE

A Siamese Tail

(Reprinted from 'Siamese News Journal')

HE WAS ALL THAT a Siamese should not be. His body round and plump, his feet rather large and his tail was short and hooked. His eyes were a beautiful blue, and, alas, they squinted somewhat. No wonder he felt a little forlorn.

Of course, his mother washed and cared for him just as much as she did his five brothers and sisters, who all gambolled and played with him quite happily. However, he had begun to realise that there was a difference between them. It began when the first visitors were allowed to see them. After exclaiming 'how sweet they are' someone noticed his tail and laughed at it. This made poor Stumpy rather ashamed of his appendage and he took to trying to tuck it out of sight when visitors came.

Yesterday a lady had purchased his sister, Sue, and was coming later today to take her to her new home. There was a trace of patronage in her manner towards Stumpy today. It was almost as if he knew that he would be the last to go.

Sue was as pretty as a picture, with ears and gaze alert as her sapphire eyes watched a fly dancing on the window pane. Her beautiful seal points shone like velvet and her tail was as straight as a whip.

Stumpy's gentle little brother, Jo.-Jo, had left yesterday to go to his new home, and as he had been his favourite brother, Stumpy was a little sad.

Mischievous Mischa, cheeky little Chu-Chu and gentle Jenny had all gone up to a 'Show' – whatever that was. He sensed that it must be very important, the biggest day in their young lives. They had been inspected and polished up, and whisked into a big wicker basket and away they had gone.

He didn't even know whether he would see them again. He'd heard the humans say that as it was nearly Christmas time, a lot of people would be looking for kittens to take home with them.

He longed for a home and humans of his very own, for he knew that these humans belonged to his mother, and he and his brothers and sisters must find their own.

He heard the door bell ringing and someone opening the door. A few seconds later the pretty young lady who had bought Sue came in with her small son.

Johnny had such a kind face that Stumpy ran to him to be petted and played with. Soon he was being cuddled and his loudest purr was coming forth. The pretty lady was telling Johnny that it was the other kitten which they were having, and see how pretty she was with her straight little tail and almond shaped blue eyes. However, Johnny was quite, quite certain that it was Stumpy whom he wanted for his very own.

He put him down on the floor with Sue and they decided to show off a little, for Siamese love to be the centre of attraction.

They knew that it always delighted the humans to see them flirt their little tails and prance sideways at each other and roll and pretend to kick and bite. Sometimes they got so excited that they did nip one another, but they always apologized.

The pretty lady was delighted with their performance and thought what a shame it would be to part them. After all, Johnny was so set on having Stumpy and she simply must have that lovely kitten for herself.

The kittens were rather tired after their exertions, and seeing a lap above them, they jumped up and settled down to sleep. How could Johnny's mother separate them now. So Stumpy had a little boy for his very own and sister Sue to play with. How happy he was at last.

CHAPTER THIRTEEN

Nursing

A N ESSENTIAL FACTOR in treating all animals, especially small animals, is gaining their confidence, and nursing is more than half the battle to be fought against whatever germ, virus or accident you have to fight.

If you are nervous, wondering if he is going to meow? Will the dose be enough? Will it be too little? Will it be too much? Can I manage it? Will I hurt him? and other conflicting thoughts, your pet will sense this indecision and reluctance and also be nervous and apprehensive.

First the temperature. A cat's normal temperature is 101.4. The correct place to take the temperature is the rectum. The thermometer enters quite easily, but cats do not like having their temperature taken and it is well to have somebody holding the patient while it is done. No force need be used; it is just a matter of holding him quietly but firmly and talking the while.

When giving medicine have everything ready. Do not wait to explain to him it is all for his own good! By that time he will have realized something is afoot – and be apprehensive. Think carefully before starting. For liquids I think the solution is the hypodermic syringe. The exact amount can be taken up in the barrel of the syringe and can literally be given drop by drop, without even moving your patient. The syringe is manipulated with one hand – you have therefore the other to stroke him, talk to him the while, thus adding to his confidence.

Cats, like humans, have their ups and downs. With regard to health, if your cat is off-colour, it is better to be sure than sorry, and call your vet at once. Even if he says there is nothing much the matter, remember some cats will not fight illness, and a day's delay in calling in professional advice could be fatal.

Cats are very sensitive to sounds; they can hear sounds we do not. Use a soothing voice when talking to your patient, but not the hushed tones of a death-bed scene, for this atmosphere will be picked up by your patient.

Always boil water when any stomach disorder is present, in adults or kittens. With kittens you cannot go far wrong if you regard your young kitten as you would a young child.

I have found that gentle but firm hand grooming is a help – while the patient is nursed take your hand from neck to tail. This grooming must not be jerky or heavy but rhythmical, thus helping the circulation and the well-being of the patient.

Night nursing of a sick animal is just as important as the day. You cannot expect your pet to respond in full if he is only given attention during your waking hours. To save his life you must make it a twenty-four hour job. This does not mean your staying up all night, but it does mean your waking at the hours prescribed for medicine, or probably having your pet in your bedroom where he has the comfort of your presence.

If perchance you have to give an enema, do take care that the soap used has no soda content. Use pure soap and warm water. There are varied types of enemas; the short type is best. Vaseline can be put on the nozzle to facilitate the entry into the rectum. Clear the bulb of the enema before using. Draw the liquid up into the rubber bulb and press until the liquid is running freely, before using.

In any illness causing discharge from a wound, eyes, nose, ears, rectum or any part of the body, keep the discharge cleaned up with a mild disinfectant. Do not get the fur wet and so cause coldness to that part of the body.

There are specially designed spoons for giving liquids. The lower end is covered in order that the fluid runs out through the small opening provided.

Anything in powder form is difficult to give unless its action is still effective if mixed with food, but here your pet may, with his delicate sense of smell, refuse to eat the food. In such cases capsules are the answer. Any unpalatable medicine can be given in them in liquid or powder. They are made by Parke Davis & Company in sizes 000, 00, 0, 1, 2, 3, 4, 5 – and they are easy to handle and administer and the whole content goes direct to the stomach.

It is often difficult to get a cat just recovering from an illness to eat, and a feeling of despondency creeps over one, having brought the patient through maybe a serious illness. Never force him to eat. Your vet can, of course, feed him during say an unconscious period with an injection in the rectum, but what can you do now. He has probably lost his sense of smell. Don't lose heart! Take a piece of sterilized cotton wool, dip in Brand's Essence or glucose and water. Wipe inside the lips and as the patient opens his mouth, as he will to lick his lips, squeeze the cotton wool, in order that he gets a little nourishment. I have found that Brand's Essence invariably brings patients on to more solid food.

A sick kitten will deteriorate in condition very rapidly, even more quickly than an adult cat. Warmth is essential in illness. By warmth I do not mean the heat of a fire or electric radiator directly on the patient. This heat does not permeate the body and is in fact liable to create a feeling of coldness on that part of the body that is away from the direct heat. Warmth, such as that given by an electric blanket, permeates the body. A waterproof sheet can be placed on top of the blanket. If you have an 'Aga' or similar cooker, these are excellent. A box can be placed on stilts on top of the stove and gentle heat is supplied to the patient. The airing cupboard is another good place, but take care that, if it is a matter of putting the patient on a shelf, care must be taken that he cannot jump and hurt himself. Do not close the door unless there is a proper circulation of air. Your own imagination will improvise something that gives a steady comforting heat night and day.

Cats that are very ill will try to crawl to a cold floor or near a door. This you must watch, for lack of warmth to the extent of a cold floor or direct draught, can result in death.

CHAPTER FOURTEEN

Feline Infectious Enteritis and Cat Distemper

I HAVE COMBINED these two complaints in one chapter, because the symptoms of the one are often confused with the other, not only by novices, but also amongst the more experienced. It will also enable me to give you a side-by-side comparison of the symptoms.

First of all Feline Infectious Enteritis. Symptoms: loss of appetite, lassitude, vomiting; when the lower part of the abdomen is touched it will be painful. The patient usually crouches and will hang over the water bowl but not drink. The vomit is greenish yellow, constipation may occur, followed by diarrhœa, with a most unpleasant smell. There is rapid loss of condition.

The symptoms are often taken for poisoning, especially amongst the average cat owner with a pet cat, who has not heard of Feline Infectious Enteritis; and it is here the danger of spreading lies, for the virus is minute and easily passes from cat to cat and can be carried on clothes, boots, hands, etc., and then outside the home – on bus, train, tube, etc. Not only can it be carried but it is definitely airborne and being spore-covered can live months in suitable temperature – away from any contact will survive for some months.

It is therefore essential that all kittens be inoculated. There was a vaccine made in England pre-1939 and now it is once more to be had. It is Fiovax. Other vaccines are available, German, New Zealand and Swiss. Their proprietary names are FEV, ENTEROVAX and GRAEUB respectively.

Do please discuss the matter with your Vet. The first three vaccines are given in two injections of 1 c.c. each at an interval of ten to fourteen days and can be administered when the kitten is six to seven weeks old. The Swiss injection for a kitten of 3 months is 2 c.c. No vaccine can carry a guarantee of absolute immunity, but the risk is very much lessened, and if your cat does develop Feline Infectious Enteritis, its chances of recovery are far, far greater.

This disease may strike cats of any age. It is, however, rare in cats over two years of age; kittens and young cats are chiefly affected. The kitten or cat to be inoculated must be perfectly healthy.

To help you have some idea of the effect – inoculation introduces dead organisms of Feline Infectious Enteritis into the blood stream of the cat. These create the production of anti-bodies, which will attack any live virus. Fourteen days is the period considered necessary for the protection by anti-bodies.

The rapid deterioration of condition, especially in kittens, is caused by the lack of white blood cells – and its other name is Panlencopenia. The blood cells carry oxygen from the lungs to the rest of the body, so you will readily see the cause of deterioration. Post-mortem results usually find the small intestine inflamed in various degrees. Dehydration is so rapid that, if you hold the skin in your hand, it will not slip back as in a healthy cat, but stay standing in a ridge. It is almost unbelievable that body fluid can be lost so quickly.

Do have a post-mortem when you lose a kitten so as to be certain death *has* been caused by Feline Infectious Enteritis. Kittens may die from what appear to be the symptoms and you may distress yourself with fear of carrying infection, etc., needlessly.

From data collected, it would appear that incubation can be as short as two days.

Treatment: It is most important to ISOLATE. Do not forcibly feed. The small intestine is too inflamed. Waste no time, call your vet. at once. Don't visit the surgery, thus risking spreading the disease. Keep warm and quiet until the vet. arrives.

Quarantine period differs. It should be at least three months; six months is better. Although I know there are those who say three weeks, be on the safe side for the sake of your own pets and those of other people.

Feline Infectious Enteritis is a virus; thus care must be taken in drugs used without the co-operation of your vet. The use of drugs could be dangerous. Penicillin is of no use in fighting the actual disease, but this and sulphonamide drugs can be most effective in coping with secondary infection.

If the patient survives 24 to 36 hours, there is a better chance of recovery. Nursing is most important. Follow your vet's directions very carefully. Should you, owing to distance or some other circumstance, be unable to get a vet. and your pet is holding his own, give glucose and water and Brand's Essence alternately, at least every hour, remembering always that he must not be allowed to lose energy. You must be 'at one' with your patient to pull with him in his fight to recover. As your pet is unable to drink, the replacement of body fluid is most important. As he picks up, advance to light diet in due course.

Your vet. will probably give 'saline injections'. The first time you see this done you will be amazed at the size of syringe and the amount that can be absorbed. Saline injections have saved the life of many a beloved pet.

The virus can be airborne. However, the chief source of infection is the patient. Take care to have an overall specially for use when with your patient, and disinfect your hands and shoes each time you leave him. You cannot be too careful.

CAT DISTEMPER

Symptoms: Appetite may vary, may even be good for a while; lassitude need not be present, but as the illness develops, depression descends on the patient – as it does with us when we have influenza. Running eyes and nose, repeated sneezing. The mucus from this sneezing will re-infect, so for this reason, and to make your patient comfortable, keep his eyes, nose and mouth swabbed with a mild disinfectant such as T.C.P. (1 in 6).

My personal view is that inoculation for Feline Infectious Enteritis also helps to combat this disease and it is a view shared by many others. As far as I know there is no specific vaccine for distemper, for there are several forms.

The disease will attack young kittens and older cats; although not regarded as a fatal illness, it is the older cats who are more likely to succumb.

Incubation varies (as with Feline Infectious Enteritis). Three to ten days would appear to be the period.

Treatment: Isolate at once. Keep warm without being overheated; keep nose and eyes free of mucus, contact your vet.

Quarantine period: At least three weeks after full recovery.

Nursing is always important, playing a great part in recovery. The patient feels miserable, snuffly and low-spirited. Keeping his nose, ears and mouth free of mucus will comfort him. Tempt him with food. Brand's Essence is very sustaining and often will lead a patient on to eating. Minced chicken or turkey in small jars can be purchased at the grocer. I have found this excellent as a follow-on for Brand's Essence.

Secondary infection, such as Bronchial Pneumonia is a danger. Care should be taken, for this may prove fatal. (See 'Pneumonia').

Chronic catarrh may remain after the patient's recovery. This is a beastly complaint and difficult to cure. As far as I am aware, there is not at the moment a specific cure. However, each year medicine advances in the treatment of small animals. Sometimes it is wise to try an inoculation with vaccine made from the mucus discharged from the patient's nose.

Building up the system is most important after both Feline Infectious Enteritis and Cat Distemper. Halibut or Cod Liver Oil, Bit.B.Iz, Metatone and numerous other preparations help to build up the physical condition, with the addition, of course, of good food, fresh air, warmth and affection.

Here is a side-by-side comparison of symptoms:

Feline Infectious Enteritis	*Cat Distemper*
Loss of appetite.	May be good, or varied.
Lassitude and rapid loss of weight.	May not show lassitude — weight will depend on food eaten.
Yellow, frothy vomit.	Does not vomit.
Abdomen painful to touch.	Not so in this case.
No running at nose and eyes, or sneezing.	Probably running at eyes and nose and sneezing.
In fatal cases death occurs within 24/48 hours.	Not usually fatal, although illness may be prolonged.
Temperature high at first, falling rapidly as illness develops.	Temperature high.

CHAPTER FIFTEEN

Common Ailments

THE INTENTION of this chapter is not that it should supersede your vet, but to indicate the symptoms of the more common ailments. It cannot be emphasized too strongly that it is dangerous to wait before calling in your vet. The first essential in *any* ailment is warmth. Do not overlook this.

Ailments, including preparation for Vet. You can be a great help to both your pet and your veterinary surgeon if you are calm, and stop and think before telephoning. Do not ring until you have details clear in your mind – even better, write down details, i.e.:

When your pet first showed signs of illness.
When he last ate – and what.
If he has vomited – colour and substance of vomit.

The cause of the trouble may be diagnosed by the excreta – a motion stool should be kept for the vet's inspection.

Should you be calling him to a queen having kittens, have these details ready before you telephone:

When she started in labour.
Date kittens due.
If it is her first litter.

Should anything occur between telephoning and his visit, make a note of it.

If you have any particular questions you wish to ask him, do write them down. He will ask questions and in the general worry of the moment, you may forget what you want to know. I have found veterinary surgeons most co-operative, but you must remember they are busy men and cannot make a social visit of each call.

Giving Medicine. First have everything ready to hand before you start; do not fuss about. Capsules and tablets are comparatively easy to give. Carefully open the cat's mouth with the thumb and first finger of your left hand, across the back of the head, firmly holding the jaw on either side. With the right hand drop the tablet into the back of the throat. Often the cat will swallow at once. In a split second you will realize if he is not going to do this. Then quickly push down with little finger. This may sound difficult, but practice will make it very simple.

Liquids are more difficult. If a spoon is used, hold the head same way, but do not open the mouth wide. Slight pressure will allow you to insert the spoon in the side of the mouth and let it dribble down.

To give oil of any kind, it is far better to warm it. It will then not only run more easily off the spoon, or whatever you use, but it will be more easily absorbed. Method: Put the required amount and a little over into a cup, place this in a saucepan of water and bring to the boil. (Do not let the water boil over into the cup). Heat sufficiently to allow the oil to liquify.

A hypodermic syringe (with needle removed) is excellent for giving liquids, for the correct amount can be drawn into the barrel and the liquid given slowly. NEVER drop liquid medicine of any kind to the back of the throat. There is no need to open the mouth wide to give liquids.

I have set the Ailments out in alphabetical order for easy reference.

Abscesses: These can form on any part of the body and are caused by the body throwing off a localized infection. Cause may be from a scratch or bite into which dirt has penetrated. The abscess should be bathed with hot salt water or just hot water. When it has burst, drain away the pus; do not allow the abscess to heal over until it is quite clear, or another will form. Should the vet have to be called, he will lance and drain.

Asthma: This is not common in cats, but comes to some older cats. Do not allow a cat with this complaint to get too fat; the bowels should be kept open and a light diet is advisable.

Bad Breath: Can be caused by stomach trouble, causing indigestion, worms or bad teeth. If the teeth are coated with tartar, this should be removed. If need be, call in your vet. Worms and stomach upsets amount to the same thing. The worms upset the stomach, thus causing bad breath. (See 'Worms').

Bronchitis: The danger here is that, if not treated at once, pleurisy or pneumonia may follow as secondary infection. The patient coughs and finds breathing difficult, often dribbles and refuses to eat. Friars Balsam can be used as an inhalant. (Six drops to a cup of boiling water.) The patient must be kept warm, but at the same time fresh air is a necessity.

Bowels: The intestines are a guide in your pet's health. The excrement or waste matter they eject gives information as to their bodily health, i.e., Constipation, Diarrhœa, Coccidiosis and other troubles which are diagnosed on examination by experts of the excreta. Under the microscope minute germs and viruses can be identified, and then treated.

Biliousness: Your pet feels just plainly 'out of sorts' – and looks it. Constipation or diarrhœa can be present. Do not bother with food – he probably will be quite fit in a day, and a day without food does not harm human or feline. There is generally a great thirst. The patient should not be allowed much water, and all water should be boiled. First meal should be light.

Broken Limbs: The setting of broken limbs is a job for the expert. Until your vet's arrival, keep the patient quiet and warm. Surgery has advanced in great strides. Nowadays limbs can be united by nut and bolt, where it is advisable. An X-ray is taken of the broken limb. Quite often this means an anæsthetic – the X-ray is through in a minute and the patient's limb set before he comes round. I have had both a cat and dog with broken legs – both have seemed actually to have enjoyed themselves and quite showed off their splinted limbs.

Blood Blisters: These are not frequent. The blister starts in the usual way, but becomes so heavy that the ears bear the head down. If draining does not suffice, your vet will, at the right moment, lance it. The muscles of the ear are likely to be affected if the blister is neglected.

(Above) *A beautiful study of Mrs. V. Seaton Reed's Lung Wha Lobelia.*

Mrs. J. C. Nicholls' Kenspeckle Balkis conveys all the dignity of a Siamese.

Siamese in South Africa. The kitten is Silverlawns Saucy Talk, a daughter of Sanguine Soniboi, and she is pictured here with Eleuthera Excellency, best Blue Point at the Rhodesia Cat Club Show, 1959. Owner Mrs. I. Taylor.

Elmham Biri Khan, Elmham Belinda and Elmham Ballerina, three lovely kittens bred by Misses Dawson and Theobald. Their dam was Elmham Linda Jem, and their sire, Doneraile Marquis.

Burns: Generally speaking, acid burns should be treated with alkali solution and alkali burns with acid solution. Warmth and quiet for the patient, to whom the shock will be great.

Choking: Can be caused by any object lodged in the throat. Usually a bone of some sort. Be very certain you can handle your patient, who will probably be frightened. You must look at the object and decide whether it is small enough to be pushed down, or taken out with forceps. It may be expedient that you tackle the removal, for your own sake and that of your pet. Be confident and quick. Well wrap up the patient in a towel and have somebody hold him so that he cannot get his feet out.

Constipation: Your cat should have a motion every day and constipation should not occur if a cat is fed a mixed diet and has plenty of exercise. This condition can be relieved by a change of diet such as liver (well-boiled), sardines, etc. If persistent, liquid medicinal paraffin or one of the patent preparations can be used. However, constipation must not be neglected or serious illness may result.

Coccidiosis: Is more usually a disease of young rabbits but does occur in cats. It is most infectious and scrupulous cleanliness should be observed. Toilet trays should be changed and disinfected after each motion, to stop infection spreading. In these days treatment with the sulphonamide drugs effects a cure. It is an infection of the intestines, the excreta being vile-smelling, yellowy and very loose.

Catarrh: Nasal inflammation of the mucous membrane. The cat is not ill but sneezes, often has running eyes and is miserable looking, although may not be off his food. Do not let this condition continue or it may develop into Snuffles (see page 83). Relief can be found in the inhaling of Friars Balsam. Rhinofagas or Fenox have also been found excellent. In the case of the latter a dropper or spray is supplied.

Colds: Always treat a cold with suspicion for it may turn into something more serious. Catch it in its early stages. Keep the patient in an even temperature, with as much fresh air as possible.

An aspirin given night and morning for the adult may fend the cold off – if not and it develops, keep the eyes, nose and throat clean with mild disinfectant, such as solution of salt and water (teaspoonful to a pint). For the throat, weak permanganate of potash and salt is excellent. Keep diet light and bowels open.

Cat Influenza: Is much like the human form. Sneezing, sickness, lassitude; there are, as in the human, many forms of the complaint. Warmth is essential. Give Brand's Essence and raw minced meat to keep up the patient's strength. Keep nose, eyes, mouth and throat clean by swabbing with disinfectant.

Canker: See 'Ears'.

Diarrhœa: A sign that something is wrong! Maybe wrong diet, or sudden change of diet. This often happens with a kitten going to his new home and raw lean meat will probably clear up the trouble. Do not give sloppy foods. Whatever the cause, it must be found. Vi Siblin (Parke Davis) can be added to the diet. This is rich in Vitamin B.

Kaolin Powder is a good stomach disinfectant but not a cure. Enterofagas, a remedy I am never without, is excellent. Bismuth Carbonate on all food will often effect a cure. Entavet, Chloromycetin, Palmitate or Terramycin Powder are two of the more modern remedies.

Dribbling: Cats will dribble to cast from their mouth a taste they dislike. It may denote bad teeth, indigestion, poison – fear, joy – or something more serious. Wipe the mouth out with mild disinfectant or even warm water.

Eczema: Is not common among cats, and is not contagious. The usual cause is wrong feeding, which causes the bloodstream to become impure, thus causing small irruptions. A change of diet will usually bring relief quite quickly.

There are two types of Eczema – DRY and WET. For both a dose of liquid paraffin, Isogel, Petrolagar or similar preparation will help to clear the poisons from the system and so help to purify the blood stream. Further treatment for Wet Eczema: Bathe any pus away and dust with sulphur powder. For Dry:

Sulphur and **Lard, or** sulphur and medicated paraffin should be applied.

Irritation is a problem. Relief can be given by bathing with soothing lotion such as one uses for sunburn. The patient must not be allowed to scratch. If need be a collar must be made of cardboard.

Cut a circular piece large enough to stop the patient scratching, make a hole in the centre, slit from the outer edge to the opening, place in position round the patient's neck and lace with strong string.

Eyes: A healthy cat has bright, clear eyes. If the haw (inner eyelid) continually partly covers the eye, the cat is out of condition (although I have known cats who seemed to be able to do this at will, when wanting attention). It is wise, however, to watch his excreta for signs of worms, for a cat cannot be in good condition if he has a worm infestation. He should improve with a course of conditioning to build him up.

For conjunctivitis and other eye trouble, there are many remedies on the market today. To name a few:—

Aureomycin ointment (Ophthalmic).
Chloromycetin ointment.
Neo-corte F 1.5% drops.
Procaine penicillin.
Terramycin (Ophthalmic).
Evan's Sodium Sulphacetamide.
Mystepton.
Albucid.
Crook's Collosal Agentum.

Some of these can only be purchased with a veterinary surgeon's prescription. All the above have been proved by breeders. However, bear in mind that, as with the human, the remedy that suits one may not suit another. So it is with your pet.

When your kittens open their eyes, you may find one whose eyes or one eye is still closed and, whereas it is not inflamed, a very fine crusty substance will be keeping the lids together – this crust is sometimes hardly visible and so you may be inclined to leave it to the kitten's mother. Don't! Bathe open with warm boracic water, or even weak cold tea, and treat with one of the eye ointments; Albucid, for instance. The time to catch any trouble is before, or at least at the start; do not let it build up.

DO NOT fly to the stronger remedies when boracic water or weak salt water with witch hazel will fit the bill and do not dabble from one remedy to another. If no improvement, call your vet.

Ears: Canker is the main trouble. It is caused by a mite which sets up irritation, causing the cat much discomfort. He will shake his head and scratch behind the ear so energetically to relieve the irritation, that his ears may become sore. It may be necessary to make a collar of cardboard to fit round his neck, thus stopping him getting his paws behind his ear. To make a collar, take a piece of cardboard large enough to stop your cat's paw reaching behind it when in place. Cut a hole in the centre, then slit from the outside edge of the opening, place in position on the neck and lace with strong string.

There are several kinds of canker; all have the same symptoms. The ear can be cleaned with weak solution of Peroxide of Hydrogen, Surgical Spirit and water, or warm Olive Oil. There are also a number of patent remedies. Mycil dusting powder has been found very effective. To clean the ears, use cotton wool rolled round an orange stick, or, even better, pick up the cotton wool with a pair of tweezers and then roll round; this holds the wool firm. Whatever you use in liquid form, do not leave the inside of the ears wet, and do not excavate! Just clean the ear out!

Fleas: See 'Parasites'.

Indigestion: Caused by taking food too quickly, or over-eating, causing wind and sickness. Enterofagas or Milk of Magnesia will give relief.

Intussception: This is an acute abdominal catastrophe caused by part of the bowel invaginating the neighbouring part. Early operation is essential to prevent gangrene of the bowel, acute obstruction, peritonitis and inevitable death. The kitten does not grow, as the digestive system breaks down. Fortunately it is of rare occurrence.

Jaundice: Is a symptom, not an illness. It is caused by the gall bladder not being able to provide the bile necessary to aid the digestion and the yellow pigment gets into the blood. Do not waste time. Call your vet.

Lice: See 'Parasites'.

Maggots: See 'Parasites'.

Parasites: *Fleas:* These do not breed on the cat. The small black grit-like particles found on the cat's coat are flea excreta – not eggs, as is sometimes thought. The fleas hatch out in dust, dirt, floor-boards and corners. They go through a cocoon stage and emerge as fleas. So that, if you find fleas on your pet, you must not think he is free after one clearance. You must comb the coat daily. Spratts make a special comb for this purpose. There are many good powders on the market – Lorexare Pulver, Pyrethrum Powder and others.

Maggots: These are rarely found on Short Hair cats. The maggots should be removed and the part bathed in disinfectant.

Lice: These do lay their eggs on the coat of the cat. Fortunately it is rare for a cat in good health to be the host of these small parasites; they are quite small, greyish in colour. Treat as for Fleas.

Ticks: These are usually picked up by cats living in the country. They are a greyish blue and hang like blisters from the cat's body. The tick has a firm hold, but do not worry; they are easily removed. Take a feather, dab in turpentine, ammonia or surgical spirit, touch the tick at the point of entrance through the skin. It will release its hold. Destroy at once. If pulled they may break and thus cause an abscess.

Pneumonia: May follow low vitality, colds, distemper, in fact any illness. Temperature rises and the breathing becomes rapid. Warmth and quiet are essential. Get your vet as quickly as possible. There are numerous drugs to fight this illness. Your vet will decide which is suitable to your pet's particular case.

Should you have to use a pneumonia jacket, do not make it too thick or so close-fitting that it is tight to the body. The jacket consists of two pieces of flannel with cotton wool or

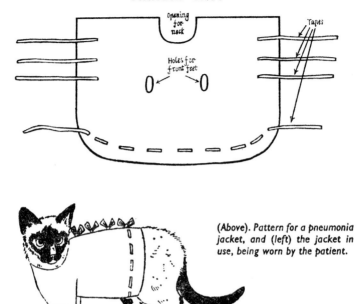

(Above). *Pattern for a pneumonia jacket, and (left) the jacket in use, being worn by the patient.*

thermogene placed between. The front paws should go through the holes and the tapes fasten along the neck.

Poisoning: Do keep poison out of reach of your animals. Fertilisers etc., if spilt on garage or potting shed floors, should be cleared up at once. Cats like to roll and may pick up something, which, when they lick their fur to clean their coats, enters the stomach. Arsenic, Strychnine and Phosphorous are all used as poisons for vermin.

Arsenic causes pain and diarrhœa, which may be coloured with blood.

Strychnine causes convulsions. Give an emetic, for it is essential to get the cat to vomit.

Phosphorus causes vomit which may be luminous. Treat with alkaline, such as soda.

General treatment as for humans: alkalis for acid poisons, acid for alkali poisons.

Rickets: Fortunately this is not a complaint one finds often in kittens. The unfortunate thing is that it is not often noticed at once. Kittens may limp after jumping – sometimes for a day. The bones are brittle, owing to lack of mineral salts and slight greenstick fractures occur, which are so slight they heal themselves. If this continually happens, consult your vet. When your queen is again in kitten, sterilised bone flour should be given. (This can be obtained from British Glue Company, Welwyn Garden City). Half a tablet of ascorbic acid, 25 mgm., morning and evening; also Halibut Liver Oil; proprietory brands of mineral salts can be obtained at your chemist.

Ringworm: Do not let anybody deter you from attempting to cure ringworm. It is a horrid complaint caused by a fungus growth which spreads from the centre outwards. Iodine is excellent but drying, and the use for too long or too much can cause poisoning. Far the best thing is not to try any remedy yourself, but call your vet. Remember that one hair will start the trouble off again, so burn everything burnable. It is also a complaint which can be passed to humans.

Snuffles: This is a most difficult condition to cure. In chronic cases, a vaccine can be made from the mucus discharged from the patient's nostril and this has been found effective, when used as an injection. See that the patient has good food, and his constitution built up. The nostril should be kept clean and a dropper or spray used regularly.

This complaint is sometimes left after distemper, bronchitis or pneumonia, or may follow a cold in the head. It can become a chronic condition. The cat breathes thickly, the nasal passages being clogged. All mucus should be wiped constantly from the nostrils; in some cases the mucus is infected but this is not always so. Better to regard it as such and see that, should you have other cats, they do not contact the patient. This is actually a chronic catarrhal condition. Use mild disinfectant when clearing mucus and keep the cat's physical constitution built up.

Stomatitis: The mucous membrane of the mouth becomes inflamed. Bad teeth may cause this condition; always beware of any inflammation, which may develop into distemper. The cat generally refuses food and ropes of saliva hang from the mouth. Wash the mouth out with T.C.P. (6 in 1). Do not take this illness lightly. The inflammation is a good breeding ground for germs, whilst the lowered condition of the patient makes resistance to germs more difficult.

Sickness: If food is vomited back, it is usually that your pet has overeaten, or eaten too quickly. White or frothy vomit may mean indigestion or gastritis in any form. All forms of indigestion are gastric upsets. However, should the vomiting continue – be wise, call your vet.

Teeth: Cats seldom suffer from toothache, but their teeth should be examined from time to time. Bad teeth will cause indigestion, and as they grow older the teeth are liable to become coated with tartar if left; this will lead to decay.

Your vet will keep the teeth scaled; it is rather a difficult job to tackle oneself and should be left to a skilled and trained hand.

Vitamins: Vitamins and mineral salts are necessary for the well-being of animals; in their wild state they find these in the various plants and small animals, birds, etc., upon which they feed.

A. & D. are Anti-Infection.

E. helps Fertility.

B. & C. are Body-Builders – beneficial to the nervous system.

H. Now considered B.5.

Vitamins can, in most cases, be purchased in tablet, capsule and liquid form; just to mention a few:

Cylacon Vit. B.12 – liquid and tablet.

Caldeferrum Vit. D. and Calcium.

Mulivite Tablets.

Abedex – is excellent for growing kittens.

The first all lilac-pointed litter to be born in Great Britain. Bred by the author they are Doneraile Druce, Dalman, Dryad, Desire and Dresden.

Miss E. Ellias' Shansa (19 months) and Browndreys Tamba (2 months).

ADMINISTERING MEDICINE
FROM A SYRINGE

(left) *The correct way of holding the syringe.*

(right) *Hold the cat comfortably in your lap.*

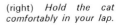

(left) *Never give the dose under the tongue.*

(right) *The correct way to insert the syringe in the cat's mouth.*

Worms: Prevention is better than cure, by taking care that all food is fresh, keeping your cat free from fleas and giving a weekly dose of garlic. Garlic is not a cure but an excellent deterrent, and can be given in capsule, tablets or liquid. I find my cats readily take Garlic Juice on their meals and suggest you make a practice one definite day each week. Kittens infected with worms cannot be expected to make headway, but do take care in treating a kitten and use nothing purging. T.C.P. is excellent – a ten days' course (again on their food) will help to keep them free.

The worms usually found in cats are Round, Thread and Tape Worms. Of these the Tape is most difficult to cure, for segments break away and new worms are formed. Fleas can be the host of tapeworm eggs; constant grooming is therefore essential. Tapeworm should be treated by your vet. These days there is no need to starve and with many pills and tablets one does not see the worms. I must confess that it was more satisfying to see worms come away, or if they did not, feel your pet was clear.

I have not given you a great number of remedies and treatments. Siamese cats are not delicate; like all animals they need fresh air, food, exercise and the companionship of the people they love.

CHAPTER SIXTEEN

Export and Import

CATS HAVE BEEN EXPORTED from Great Britain for many years and some breeders are quite used to the many formalities to be observed in the different countries.

If you have not already exported a cat, remember buyers overseas want British-bred Siamese because they are known to be the best in the world. See that the buyer is not disappointed, only export the best. I have exported my 'Doneraile' Siamese to many countries including Germany, Holland, Belgium, Sweden, Canada, Australia, Kenya, Malaya, Argentina and many to the U.S.A. I have always exported the best possible stock and done everything to maintain the high British standard. As a result of this policy, I am rewarded by the satisfaction of the importers in that my exported stock have attained Championship and International Championships, Best in Shows and other Awards.

In some countries an Import Licence is required. See that you have the licence form from the purchaser before the cat is dispatched, otherwise it may be refused entry.

In these days, when most cats are sent by air, it is important to ensure that the cat travels in a proper container. For many years Spratts Limited have supplied me with export containers, made of light wood, with a hinged feeding tray and a half-wire door. It is light in weight and is draught-proof with ample air circulation. Cats imported into this country or returning with their owners from overseas must spend six months in quarantine. Addresses of authorised accommodation can be obtained from the Ministry of Agriculture & Fisheries. The animal is collected at the ship-side or airport and transferred to the quarantine, under veterinary supervision. If you are returning to England with your cat, make all the necessary arrangements beforehand.

Cat Clubs and Welfare Organisations

IN ENGLAND both Pedigree Cats and Household Pets are well catered for by a number of Cat Clubs in London and the provinces; some of these Clubs are for special breeds of cats and others cater for all of the breeds. There are several voluntary organizations which care for the interests of Household Pets and the many other cats without homes found on bomb sites and in the streets. The functions of Cat Clubs are to encourage the breeding of Pedigree stock and to improve standards by the promotion of Cat Shows. During the past twenty years the number of Cat breeders in England has more than doubled, and although there has been a tremendous increase in the number of cats bred, the keen competition at Cat Shows has undoubtedly done much to maintain the standards. The attendance of the public at the Shows has also shown a marked improvement and although the primary object in organizing Shows is the improvement of the breeding standards, it is encouraging to find the interest in pedigree cats increasing year by year.

The Cats' Protection League, whose headquarters are at 29 Church Street, Slough, is the only organization supported by public subscription, which is, as its title implies, entirely devoted to the welfare of Cats. For many years the organization has done much to encourage a better understanding of cats. The Society issues educational literature in booklet form under the title *Some Facts About Cats* and publishes for its members, a magazine called *The Cat;* this is perhaps the oldest magazine devoted to cat welfare only. Membership of The Cats' Protection League costs one guinea per annum and is open to any person who has the welfare of cats at heart. Write to the Secretary, The Cats' Protection League, 29 Church Street, Slough, Bucks., who will be pleased to furnish details of the Societys' work, and particulars of membership.

The People's Dispensary for Sick Animals is a veterinary organization which cares for the health of all small animals, whose owners are unable to afford private veterinary service. Its dispensaries can be found in all parts of London and the Provinces. These dispensaries are staffed by veterinary Practitioners and others who provide expert advice and medical attention to all animals, free of charge. This Society does excellent work in the care of all small animals and well deserves the financial support and sympathy of all cat lovers. Collection boxes are provided at all its dispensaries and donations will be welcomed by the Secretary, People's Dispensary for Sick Animals, 31 Cork Street, London, W.1, who will also supply full details of its work.

The Royal Society for the Prevention of Cruelty to Animals is interested in all animals, large and small. It is constantly alert with regard to their welfare and few weeks pass without some reference in the National Press to its animal rescue work in some form or another. At its dispensaries treatment is free and its Inspectors are located up and down the country. It is supported by public subscription. Information regarding its wrok can be obtained from the Headquarters, R.S.P.C.A., 105 Jermyn Street, London, S.W.1.

The Universities' Federation of Animal Welfare is somewhat different from the others I have mentioned. Its basic function is to obtain authentic knowledge relating to the welfare of animals and to convey this knowledge to those who can best use it advantageously. This is done partly by research and partly by contact with a wider body of experts.

Lecturettes can be obtained from its headquarters. For children, *The Cat* by Frances Bellerly, is excellent; it is so comprehensive. Of Siamese she says: 'Siamese, lovely smooth creatures cream-coloured with mask, faces, ears, feet and tail looking burnt, and blue eyes'. This lecturette would interest not only children, but all lovers of cats whatever their age.

The Universities' Federation for Animal Welfare's address is, 7a Lamb's Conduit Passage, London, W.C.1.

ALL THAT GLITTERS

Some girls have lots of diamonds
    And two mink coats apiece;
They drive about in Bentleys,
    And sun themselves in Nice.
Admirers bring them orchids
    To match their Dior dresses;
But under all the glamour
    Their lives are full of stresses.
For mink can get the moth in,
    And gentlemen are fickle;
And if they lose their diamonds too
    They're in a proper pickle.
So I am very lucky
    Not to have such cares as these;
The only thing *I* dread to lose
    IS MY SIAMESE.

K. W. D.

Index